JACQUELINE KENT

You've Got This!

Self-Help made Simple

First published by Mirrored Publications 2021

First edition

ISBN: 9781916425842

This book was professionally typeset on Reedsy.
Find out more at reedsy.com

To the man of my dreams, my fiancé Bruce.

I will never be able to thank you enough
for the support you have shown me and my boys,
for the strength of your belief in me,
and for the love and laughter you share with us,
every single day.

Thank you
xxxx

ps. I love YOU more

Contents

Introduction: A Love note from me to you

Hello!

I'm thrilled that you've picked up this book on a hunt for something powerful and uplifting to help you out of a sticky spot in your life. I am sure you won't be disappointed. I share lessons from a place of survival, having bounced back from many of life's trials and disappointments, and now helping others with the lessons it has taught me, All too often I have brought myself out of a place of darkness and solitude by doing just the things talked about in this book.

Over some 25 or more years I have tried and tested many and varied forms of self-help activities, from creative hobbies to meditation and mindfulness, and before I began my writing career in 2018, I already had the intention of sharing this journey to help others. In almost 3 decades of my life, since the young age of 16, I have been faced with many trials and traumas, and have survived every single one, the majority of it without any medical intervention.

In my first book *Onward and Upward* I share much about the journey I have been on, I talk about some of those experiences, how they affected me, how I 'coped' (I'm still not entirely sure that's the right word!), and what kept me going. I share how I found my way to live a much happier life, and the techniques discussed here also featured briefly in that because they are how I am still standing.

And so to this book.

Packed with real, relatable accounts of all the different ways I have found the strength to 'keep calm and carry on' - if you pardon the cliché. There have been days when I have not had the answers - not any of them - to the challenges life has presented me with, sometimes new ones daily – and there have been days when I just don't care anymore. About anything. So many times I have heard the words 'I don't know how you did that?', 'How did you cope with such a tragedy?', 'How are you still smiling?' Well, I am. I don't quite know how either, to be honest.

But I need to share these coping strategies with you. Each of them is tried and tested, in the sense that I have used or at least begun to learn how they can help. In some cases, just finding out how I could help myself was enough, sometimes just the focus of feeling I was doing something positive to lift me did the job. Every single one of us is different, and everyone can find their own interpretation of what I am about to share with you. I have so much to share, that it seems rude not to. My hope in picking up this book is that you will find a truth somehow relatable to your own, which I can gently guide you through. Maybe you are struggling with loneliness and isolation, on a journey to find yourself, feeling really 'blah' about your life - perhaps you are in an unfulfilling relationship and know that you deserve something more. I have been there. I have 'self-helped' (is that a word? I guess so, as I just made it one) myself through so many varying degrees of difficulty, and at each stage, I just wished I had someone I could call on who would tell me what I needed to do.

I hope to help you find the courage to face another day, no matter how tough that seems right now. Please just trust me when I say I have been there.

Sometimes, our tanks run on empty. We can struggle to remember how to breathe, how to speak, how to think for ourselves. If you have picked up this book, I know you know what I mean.

At the time of writing this section of the book, I am feeling exactly like that. We have faced a lot of challenges in the time that no one will forget in a hurry – Covid-19. Not just thanks to a global pandemic, but also due to other more personal challenges my tank is running on empty and I am tired. It's feeling like that which reminds me that it's time to do something more about it than 'just' pick myself up and dust myself down, yet again. I know I will make it, hell I have made it through much worse – I am a survivor, but I want to help others learn to do it too. In recent days, I have reminded myself time and time again that is isn't just down to my mental strength, I have things I can draw on that will help get me through, and in doing them I will be able to share with you exactly how you can do the same.

Using my Heartfelt Approach

Towards a more fulfilling life, which encompasses the ideals of Honouring yourself, Embracing opportunities and new situations, Aligning yourself with everything that feels more 'you', Realising your dreams to lead you to a Thriving life (spells out the word HEART, do you like?) you will slowly begin to see a change in how you feel within.

I don't offer any guarantees that you will 'get over' whatever it is that you are struggling with, most of what I am about to share is most certainly *not* a prescription available on the NHS, but it might just set you on the right path. Not any one of these strategies is necessarily something that needs to belong forever, in some cases you may find you don't like what I am sharing at all, but there truly is something in this book for everyone, whether you need a little help or a lot. I hope you find the answers you are looking for.

If you are not sure where to start, just close your eyes and open it at a random page – you never know what you might discover!

Ready?

With my heartfelt admiration,

Jacqueline x

How to read this book

First of all

I want you to know that this book is not intended as some kind of instruction manual, where you read through the instructions from start to finish and by the end, you know EXACTLY what you need to do to feel better.

That probably won't work for you. If you're anything like me, you like to dip in and out of things and cherry-pick whatever takes your fancy (a bit like the tracklisting on an album - I hardly ever listen to them from beginning to end any more! I always like to mix things up a bit and click the 'random' order button! Ask anyone who knows me, I can be a little 'random' myself).

It's completely intended as the kind of book you can just 'dip' into as you need, maybe there's something that hits the spot and you have been investigating it for yourself but want to see what an impact it had on the life of another? Go ahead, choose your chapter and find out exactly how I have survived everything from teen pregnancy to mum's worst nightmare, from domestic abuse to parenting my son with a disability, bringing us to the here and now of mentally crafting my way through a global pandemic!

It all happened to me and I am here to tell the tale. Enjoy (if that is even the right word!), and I hope that you find something, even just one small thing you can take away from this to begin to find your way forward.

You are warmly invited to look through the chapter listing and choose one that speaks to your soul. I have designed it that way because there is never a one size fits all approach to looking after your wellbeing and your mental health. This is why I have called the chapters exactly what they are about, so there can be no confusion over what it is you are about to dip into.

To help you find your way, this book is gently divided into 2 sections.

Are you more of a practical action-taker, or a heart-led spiritual being?

The first section is more intended for those of you who need a little support while you take the first steps with self-care. Maybe you have only just come to realise that it's long overdue, it's time to bump yourself up the list and you don't know where to start? That was me, once upon a time, a tired mum without a minute to herself and not enough of that to go around either. Once I began to prioritise that, I soon saw a noticeable difference between the 'old' me, and the happier, more relaxed newbie. I use my unique Heartfelt Approach to help you carefully take consistent steps towards taking better care of you, because that's where it all starts!

The second section promises just a sprinkling of spirituality, nothing heavy, but is intended to give you a few more pointers about techniques you can look into, should you wish, which promise to guide you on the way to digging a little deeper and beginning to find your true self. Maybe you have already tried the gentler approach and are ready to truly go for it, applying yourself to something that offers a more holistic way of thinking – who knows where it will lead! I never imagined when I started on the latest phase of my journey in 2016 that I would eventually come to understand the Law of Attraction more fully and embrace it more freely or even go ahead and get myself a level 1 Reiki certification! All of these lead to many wonderful things as you are soon to find out when you turn the page.

When you are reading, I suggest you do so with an open mind. I am not here to preach or tell you how to think, I am merely sharing with you things I have learnt that have really and truly given me a much brighter future with hope for so much more to come and I am so glad I learned them when I did.

Also worth noting:

Every chapter in this book has an accompanying exercise in my free PDF workbook:

Visit **bit.ly/YGTworkbook** to get your copy now!

If you are still not sure where to start, check out the chapter simply called 'Just start', which will help you work out for yourself what you can do to begin. I've kept it nice and simple because I understand completely that overwhelm can be one of the biggest causes of putting something off.

Why not grab yourself a cuppa and take a look at that chapter now.

Just start…

A short list of things you can start doing today to begin to make a difference.

Where to begin? Let's keep it simple.

Slow down.

You probably have a hundred thoughts whirring round in your head right now, and it's draining you fast. Stop whatever it is you're doing and observe. Just be, for a moment (I realise now the irony in calling this chapter 'Start' then telling you to stop something! Hey, I'm just human).

Give yourself a break!

You're a human 'being', not a human doing. Our expectations that we put on ourselves, more often than not, can be the most critical thoughts we will face in our daily lives. You are the only person you are guaranteed to spend every single day of the rest of your life with, so be kinder to yourself, you've got a long road ahead together. Think about how you would support a friend, if you felt they were being too hard on themselves. You wouldn't be as harsh as you are with yourself, would you? So how is it okay to be so self-critical to the most important being in your world (that's you, by the way)? A really simple way to start doing this is by trying not to use the word 'should'. Sounds simple enough (maybe too simple?) – how often have you listened to the monologue that says 'I really *should* be busier/more fun/more serious/earning more money/less frivolous/kinder/more of something else' – we've all done it. What if that word didn't even exist?

Breathe.

Remembering this very basic function can be quite useful, we may take it for granted but if you just did that and nothing else, even for a few minutes, you would probably notice your heart rate decrease, and other things that felt completely too much right now would slowly start to dissipate. They don't go away, but you would feel more like you can break them down into manageable chunks. If you are feeling at all panicky, you can use the 7/11 technique*. Breathe into your stomach for the count of 7 through your nose, and out for the count of 11 through your mouth. This will restore the balance of oxygen vs carbon dioxide, producing a response in your body which physically lowers your anxiety, and help you to feel calmer/more in control.

Prioritise.

What's the worst that can happen if that thing you are struggling to complete doesn't get done? Is it really a matter of life or death? Or does it just feel like it, because you've been putting off doing it for so long? Can you choose something that will give you a better feeling or mindset, even just for a tiny while? Even just 5 minutes?

Take a step back.

If you just step away from something, whether it be a situation, conversation, project, or anything else that's stressing you out, maybe for a half-hour cuppa break, for an afternoon or longer, you can regain some clarity, calm your mind a little, and return to it when you are ready. Sometimes these things are sent to try us, it might be that you realise you don't need to be spending so much energy on it anyway, or perhaps it just makes its way off the 'to-do' list because it was a crazy idea you didn't need to follow up on in the first place. Whatever it is, I hope that by moving yourself away for a wee while you can start to realise that being kinder to yourself is always going to make a difference. Always.

As Louise Hay said 'You've been criticising yourself for years and it hasn't worked. Try approving of yourself and see what happens.'

Choose just one of these things you can do right now, in this moment - give it a go and see for yourself.

You've got this!

**You can find more information from the source of this technique in the useful info section at the end of the book.*

Just stop...

A quick burst of things you can stop doing right now to get out of your own way.*

Don't

let the mind monkeys get the better of you – those little voices of your own that dumb you down? Tell them to go away. Name them if that helps. Swear at them if you really need to!

Don't

let those well-meaning relatives and friends-of-friends tell you you're doing it (whatever it is) 'wrong'.

Stop

playing the shame game – you have suffered enough.

Don't

lead your life based on how you see other people doing their 'thing'. It's their thing, not yours.

Don't

waste essential energy beating yourself up mentally over all the things you're <u>not</u> currently doing.

Stop

putting down those things you always wanted just because you don't believe you're good enough. *You are enough, you have always been enough.*

Don't listen

to the world and his wife tell you their story so you can feel better about your personal hell. What you're living through is real, it's hardgoing and you deserve to make your own way.

Stop worrying

that you're never going to do it as well as Sheila or Donna from down the road, or that you shouldn't be doing it in the first place because you're not informed/learned enough - that's called imposter syndrome. We all have a version of it, and none of it is real.

Don't compare

your relationship to someone else's. your pain or suffering to that of another. Your beginning to someone else's middle, or ending.

Stop

allowing other people's stories to prevent you from celebrating <u>your</u> good things – whatever they are, you deserve them!

Stop

doing anything that doesn't make you feel good. It isn't meant for you at this time.

I hope you can find at least one tiny tidbit on this list that resonates - just bringing your attention to a nice and simple way of being kinder to yourself, without *really* doing anything.

You've got this!

**Get out of my own way? What now?*

It does what it says on the tin. All too often we prevent ourselves from becoming the most amazing form of ourselves, by blocking or simply not doing the very thing which can help us evolve. Keep an open mind - I can't wait to hear what you discover as result!

Self care, Self preservation

Don't leave your 'self' on the shelf.

This is going to sound cheesy, and I expect you have heard it before.

Self-care is absolutely fundamental when taking care of yourself (sort of does what it says on the label). It can be life-changing.

If you prioritise yourself, it makes everything else so much easier. That is going to sound alien to you – I know it does, because it sounded the same to me, once upon a time.

Over the years, I have always given myself little pockets of 'me' time, but they haven't been particularly dedicated, to be honest. Not to start with anyway.

Having a child at 16, my 'self-care' was to always try and finish a cup of tea before it went cold. Hah, if you are a parent, you will know that is an achievement all of its own. It's a constant struggle, a little person is demanding all your time and energy, you'll be lucky if you get more than 5 minutes in the shower by yourself once or maybe if you're really lucky more than once a week.

Take this part seriously though and bit by bit, other things will slowly start to fall into place. It doesn't have to be anything big or expensive, like 3 days in a spa, or pampering and preening at every opportunity. Choose one thing, however small, that makes you feel good. Treat yourself to that. Whether it is a quiet coffee, watching the world go by in the local café (outside of lockdown this will feel easier! Anyway, I digress...), or a mindful walk, just 20 minutes with your own thoughts to clear away the cobwebs.

Try to do this one thing regularly – we are not being unrealistic here, I don't mean every day. To start with, aim for once a week or fortnight if that feels more achievable. Make it easy and then there are no excuses.

By making your needs a priority (and yes, it is absolutely okay to do this, you don't NEED permission, however, if you are seeking it, you have mine too!) you are sending a strong message out to the world that you matter. As you start to realise that it's okay for you to feel important in your own life, your self worth increases, and how others see you will also start to shift. It's quite magical to experience, you won't believe it until you see it yourself, but it is true.

It's a well-known fact that sometimes those who have been strong for too long are the ones to suffer in silence because they are so used to having to be strong. It's that 'having to be' thing – we 'have to be' so many things, as a mum, wife, business owner, employee, friend you can rely on, that we sometimes just forget what we WANT or need to be for ourselves!

'The best way to find yourself is to lose yourself in the service of others.' – Mahatma Ghandi.

My self-care journey started which kickstarted my way back to happiness began in 2012. I was experiencing a major dip.

I had been gifted some money by my mum, with the strict instruction it was to be used on something 'for me'. It was time to begin. I couldn't carry on thinking myself into overwhelm, feeling burnt out, feeling down, just wondering what the fuck was the point, actually. I had been on a journey for a long time of holding everyone else together, time and time again, so I graciously accepted.

I decided it was time to join my local gym – I made it SO simple doing this, I had to walk past it almost every day on my regular post office runs, it was so near it was ridiculous, and best of all, it was women only, which suited me just fine. I kitted myself out with appropriate attire, new trainers, clothes that made me feel like I was 'ready'. I had already lost a stone in weight by this time but I wanted to shift more.

It wasn't about the weight, it was most definitely about how I was feeling, in my mind. I had no time for exercise in my routine and it was needed. My youngest was in full-time school by now, so there wasn't really any excuse (although I've always had that 'too busy' story flying around in my head - sound familiar?). So, a quick 30-minute rotation on the various machines at the gym, 3 times a week, and I began to feel the fog lifting. It wasn't immediate, of course it wasn't, but I started then to notice the difference if I didn't manage to go for a few days – which still happened. But the message I was telling myself was that I am important - don't we all need to hear that?

Over a couple of years, my routine evolved, and I began studying mixed martial arts. It was at a family orientated centre – also very nearby. The thing about this place was that we had many options about when we trained there, I went to classes with my lads, which was great most of the time but I will be honest trying to focus your mind when you have a younger child like a flea in your ear complaining that he can't do this stretch or that move, can be a little distracting! On the whole, it was a brilliant move as the exercises were very varied and it really cleared the fog. It did a lot for my confidence too, I began to believe in myself a bit more. Here I was, learning a brand new 'thing' in my late 30s, while spending time with my lads too, and I had the goal of getting myself through the belt gradings – which were quite something! I got as far as a purple belt in my newfound skill (that's not all that far away from a black belt, not bad eh?).

As I demonstrate the various ways in which I have prioritised myself over the years, I hope you start to feel that you can do it too – think of me as your cheerleader geeing you on from the sidelines. I have tried so many different things, but these, in particular, were all slowly leading me in the right direction. I see that now.

Also vitally important on your journey of self-discovery is this – what people tell you about your choices isn't your problem. You might hear things like 'how on earth do you find the time?' (that will trigger the mind monkeys that tell you yes how exactly am I supposed to find the time to do this, I am so selfish!) or 'that sounds expensive', 'lucky you, I can't do that, my husband would never agree to it/we can't afford it/my kids' activities come first…'.

So what??? This does not mean you put your needs above those of your children, your relationship or your home-life, but you are accepting that what you need is ALSO important - vital in fact.

This is not about them. None of it is. Too many times I have wavered on my decisions to start something new, or pursue something I love, because of things that were said to me around the time. Did I regret not continuing? Most definitely.

Tell you what, I will give you a quick overview of the rest of my journey now, so you can see what magic happened when I put myself first.

In 2014, I listened to Sane New World by Ruby Wax, I used to have it on in the background while I worked on my business. It's an exceptional book to help you understand the principles of mindfulness, but I will come back to that later. It really helped me to see the benefits behind focusing my mind and slowing it down, instead of listening to negative nelly self-doubt on repeat.

I reached a pivotal point in my life that Christmas, my life as I knew it was turned on its head, and single parenthood soon began. As you can imagine, I didn't get to prioritise myself, for quite a while. I had a 17-year-old with Asperger's syndrome (a form of autism), suffering all pitfalls with his college education and serious self-esteem and anxiety issues, and an 8-year-old also struggling, adjusting to the way things are now with mummy and daddy no longer living together.

Self-care wasn't even on my radar. It can come and go like that, you see.

Over an extended period, life was changing daily, and I was completely frazzled by the whole thing. I was soon to have a life-changing coaching session with Emily who was soon to become my life coach. It was August 2016 and I was just done in, my life had got so complicated.

I don't remember the whole conversation, I remember her starting with 'tell me about your life today' – well, that was a proper laugh out loud moment, I was SO disappointed in myself for not feeling more positive - but I clearly remember her insistence that if I put my happiness and peace of mind first, everything else would fall into place.

You what? How does that work? I was in a last-ditch attempt to revive my failing marriage, I couldn't even leave my sons in the same room without supervision after an argument went wrong… Every single day was just so bloody hard, how could putting me first make a difference? How could it even be a thing?

I didn't believe her but agreed to give it a go. Daydream a little bit about what I wanted my life to look like, to feel like, dotting constant reminders on post-it notes all around my house (to this day I still have one in my bathroom cabinet!) and repeat them to myself several times a DAY. It sounds like a large undertaking but I took it in good faith and so it began.

Would you believe me if I told you that it took just 2 months for my entire world to change shape completely? 2 months, and as if by magic, I had a brand new outlook. I wasn't doing anything that different, but I had put my happiness at the top of the list.

In part, this was because all I worried about before was keeping everyone else happy with my choices, and in my heart, they weren't what I wanted, not anymore. The marriage I had worked my arse off to try and save just wasn't happening, if anything it felt as though we had started going backward, and I just couldn't do it anymore. Enough was enough.

I was seeking answers, and so I started to put it out there that I needed a solution. I had no idea who I was talking to about this – I was just saying it out loud 'please give me a solution, I need something to change, I need answers'.

I truly believe that what I did was send a kick-arse message to the universe to LIVE my life once more. I don't mean I was signing up for bungee jumps and charity hikes up Macchu Picchu, nothing quite that dramatic, but I was almost instantly thinking differently, that it was okay to think about MY future on MY terms. It was an incredibly empowering feeling. All of a sudden, those negative influences in my life didn't matter as much. If it wasn't of my choosing, I wasn't interested anymore.

My whole life began to change shape from that day, in 2016, that is the truth – I am now living a much more fulfilling, happier life with the absolute love of my life. I have a big smile on my face every day and am genuinely one of the happiest people I know! I am doing so much more than just existing now, I am living my life, I stand tall, I stand proud – some might even say I shine brighter than ever before. Considering there were many occasions I thought I may not make it with my marbles intact, that says everything for me.

A great exercise for you to do after reading this is the following:

Get a piece of paper (or visit **bit.ly/YGTworkbook t**o grab your FREE workbook) and grab a pen.

In a few quiet moments, don't think too hard but write down any ideas that come to you about how you could manage to carve out some time for yourself. Don't filter ANYTHING, write them all down. Just keep writing until you run out of ideas. You might be influenced by what you see other people doing, perhaps you have heard one of your friends say something they do and you've thought ooh I'd love to try that - put it down.

It may mean you set your alarm 30 minutes earlier to 'steal' yourself some time – just do that. Get a nice list of ideas together, then begin to map out those which require a small amount of effort, and those which might need a bit more planning.

Are they expensive hobbies?

Let's change this question before you answer it.

Are you worth investing in?

Do they require some kind of learning, training, or other input?

That's no problem at all, the internet is a vast expanse of helpful knowledge and resources!

But if you are just starting out you want something simple, relatively quick to do, and realistically affordable, just to get started.

When you have this list in front of you, I can just bet you are now starting to think a bit bigger, aren't you?

Now choose just one of those things. Get your diary and write down the day you are going to do that thing – or better still, do it today! Make a promise to yourself to do whatever it is, for you. Those around you will benefit, for sure (this is an amazing side effect of self-care, however unlikely it sounds).

A key point for feeling good, in finding your way to a regular self-care routine is this: *DO SOMETHING YOU ENJOY.*

This is sooo important. Don't do what you think you are 'supposed' to do when demonstrating self-care. Think of something that lifts you. Whether it's dance lessons, creative exploits, pamper sessions, or maybe learning a new hobby. The actual thing you decide on really isn't that important, to be honest. Especially if you are trying to just make it a new part of your routine. Start small.

Whatever you do, please just start somewhere. I am begging you because I know how hard it can be to just get started – think of this as your friendly nudge in the right direction. You have picked this book up for a reason – haven't you?

What is self-preservation?

Wikipedia quote: "Self-preservation is essentially the process of an organism preventing itself from being harmed or killed and is considered a basic instinct in most organisms."

Simply put, the art of self-preservation is the first thing you can do to protect yourself from anything which doesn't serve you or help you move forward.

What does that mean?

Maybe you have a friendship with someone who drains you. Perhaps you are in a relationship that makes you feel like you are not enough. Or maybe those nagging little voices in your head have just become so loud that you can't switch off from them.

Ask yourself first of all, what is the simplest answer to this?

It is usually simpler than we might like to think – we have a habit of over-complicating things when they seem too difficult, we put obstacles in our path to prevent ourselves from inevitable growth. This in itself can be incredibly destructive.

Take a look for one moment at a situation that just jumped into your head when you started reading this chapter. I bet there is one staring you in the face. Can you remove yourself from it, just even a little bit?

Say for example it is a toxic friendship or relationship (not necessarily romantic) which you know is doing you no good. This person drains your resources and leaves you feeling less-than about things in your life when actually you started to feel like you were getting it together. It won't be anything you have done, but you need to take a step back, for your own sanity. Stop giving so much of your valuable self to it.

Can you do this?

It might be something as simple as not responding to their messages, not reading them the second they get in contact, not answering all their calls – you don't have to cut them off completely, but I know from my own experiences of situations like this that it needs to be done. The freedom we find in allowing ourselves that tiny little bit of extra peace in our day can sometimes make all the difference.

Just think to yourself, if you feel tempted to 'help' them some more, what will happen if you don't? I bet the outcome isn't all that bad. You deserve this peace, and some people don't really know how to be 'helped', they don't really think they need it, and just suck the life out of you instead.

It might sound harsh, but many people are sent to teach us something, and if that something is to show you how to find more balance in your world, then they are already serving their purpose – but what about yours? At the cost of your sanity?

I know too well how it can feel when you have that kind of one-way street friendship, it feels like every conversation is to show some form of 'one-upmanship'. Your phone pings and you feel your heart sink, what now? Can't I just have 5 minutes to think for myself without feeling like I have to be providing this vampire with something they need?

It happened to me not that long ago, I had this friendship that ran all my reserves dry, I had no time for the people who were important because of this one person who seemed to fill my days and nights with their woes. I would feel bad if I didn't respond to their negative drawl, but couldn't seem to give myself enough space from them in between times to build up my reserves, or more importantly, handle it more effectively.

I started working on preserving my own energy as a priority, and when I did, I almost accidentally permitted myself to not respond anymore. This particular person was also on a spiritual journey of their own, however, it did not feel in alignment with mine and when I took my time to explain that battling with their negativity was undoing all my hard work, the apology came in the form of another 'poor-me' episode.

Don't get me wrong in this, I am as compassionate as they come, I am a good listener, I try to help people work their way through things, but I knew it was time. My work here was done, it was very strange but I never contacted them again and they didn't attempt to contact me. I had served my purpose for them and that is fine by me.

Perhaps you have never found yourself in the position to feel as though this is what you 'should' be doing, but sometimes you do have to assess whether what is going on is something that will ever benefit you in some way – not in a selfish way but in the form of an exchange of your energy, good energy feeds more good energy and if you are constantly being met with the lower vibrational stuff it will be hard to break free. Even with a friend who supposedly understood all this stuff, something happened that day that made me realise not everything has to be negotiated, sometimes it just ends.

When my marriage ended, after many months of trying to make it work, following some tough times, I knew I had tried everything, counselling, time apart, talking, not talking, we just kept going round in circles. One day, we just agreed it was time to reassess, and that was that. We had already said everything there could possibly be to say, I think, and I knew in my heart that it had no future anymore. Did we need to pick over the bones of what was left just to make ourselves feel like we had ended it 'properly'? No. We just agreed that this was it and it was time to close the door. It was hands down the most liberating experience of my life. But this was only possible because I accepted that my feelings mattered. I saved myself any more anguish.

After years of inner torment, struggling to understand why I never had that happy-ever-after I once sought, and instead found myself constantly questioning what it was all about, all of a sudden I was released from the burden, free to find myself and understand what I really wanted from my life. It was like I was on drugs – good ones (not something I can relate to other than those which you are given during labour and childbirth!). If this is something you daydream about, maybe you need to reassess how you can remove enough of yourself to breathe again – it doesn't necessarily mean the end of something, usually, it signifies the beginning of something else, instead (they don't have to be the same thing).

Does this help? I hope so.

I was fortunate to be gifted an empowering, real-life story book when I was in my darkest depths, I like to think that somewhere in there something triggered helping me understand just what I needed to do to get a bit of 'me' back, because ultimately I feel that is what is often missing when lost souls start on their journey of rediscovery. You feel disconnected from yourself somehow, and don't know how to find the way back.

There is a way – there is always a way.

You've got this!

BONUS MATERIAL!!!

If you enjoyed the exercise at the end of the self-care section in this chapter, I've got some great news for you!

There's plenty more where that came from!

Visit **bit.ly/YGTworkbook**

Where you can download your very own fully complimentary PDF workbook with simple exercises you can do to accompany each and every section of this book! They will help you get clear on what you need to do right now to better support yourself – and I'll be there cheering you on.

Good old fashioned Fresh air and Exercise

Before you read

What I have to say about fresh air and exercise, I just want you to know – *I am no exercise addict!* I have gone through phases of it at various stages in my life, from regular swimming and aerobics classes to pursuing a black belt in martial arts. However, at this moment in time, I feel a little more restricted in my choices, due to some physical issues I've been experiencing.

I'm telling you this because I don't ever want you to think you're being judged in any way - for anything, but in this instance – because maybe you don't currently have any kind of fitness regime. We have all been there. You may be feeling completely stuck as you pick up this book, which is the whole purpose of it – helping you find a simple solution to whatever is holding you back – something you can incorporate easily into your life.

With that in mind, I shall continue...

It's time to get yourself moving

Stagnant energy with nowhere to go does no one any good.

Simple exercise options can often be the best, especially if you are trying to incorporate them seamlessly into your life. There is nothing like a nice walk out in the fresh air to clear away the cobwebs. It's the simplest option if you are struggling, or ready to make a change. And best of all, it's free.

You have so many options to get started. Choose an area you like to walk in, with scenery that lifts your spirits. You can opt-out of technology altogether in this moment, as I love to do sometimes – leave your phone at home and just 'be'. If you love music, put on some headphones and just walk (if possible, set your phone to 'do not disturb' or take an iPod and give your headspace a complete break). Walk it out. I am not saying by any stretch of the imagination that it will cure everything, but it can just help you reset yourself a bit.

As you are walking, just focus on your steps – one foot in front of the other (an excellent mantra to adopt if you are struggling in any way). A rhythmical foot-stepping action where all you are thinking about is what you are doing at that moment – incorporating a bit of mindfulness into the bargain, double win!

I am writing this at a time when all of these things we once took for granted aren't quite so simple.

We are in the middle of Covid-19, a global pandemic, and some of our freedom has been taken away. During this time, we have only been allowed out of the house for specific things, to get a small amount of daily exercise such as a walk or run outdoors, or to get essential food shopping. It seems impossible to imagine that unless you too have been living through it. I know of so many people who truly embraced this opportunity, to get their daily exercise in whatever possible way they could. I think for the first fortnight of lockdown v1 I did the same. And then as a family, we took the stance just to ride the storm – heads down and make the most of the space immediately around us. Luckily, so far we have all remained fairly upbeat. Of course, we have had our up and down days, it's the most bizarre situation ever and undoubtedly one that will be written and read about for many years.

I struggled a fair bit in early lockdown days with anxiety, but I continued to do some of the things you will come to read about in this book, to maintain some kind of equilibrium and keep going.

Had my mental health suffered as a result of not going for regular exercise, I would have made it my non-negotiable to factor that into my day, we all would have. But we lucky, we have been solid as a family unit. We all get on pretty well, happy in our space, and without any kind of crossed wires or friction (this is an achievement in itself compared to the world I used to live in before finding my fiancé Bruce) we co-exist quite calmly and don't get under each other's feet.

Back to the exercise.

We live in a town house, with a basement level which has our kitchen and home bar in it, then 2 reception rooms on the next floor, with 2 bedrooms and a bathroom on the 'proper' first floor and a converted attic room above that – that's 4 storeys! I always felt that having so many flights of stairs left few options but to go up or down them during the day to get to either the bathroom or the kitchen must have made something of a difference in my fitness over the years – we have one very steep flight which everyone complains about when they visit - how do you do this every day? Having lived in this house for over 11 years now, I barely think about it anymore. I try to run up them as much as possible, with the hair-brained notion that it's enough exercise to be getting on with

But if I'm a bit fed up I just can't sit still, I have to keep moving somehow. During the early stages of the pandemic we were fortunate enough to make the most of our outdoor space in the back garden, I think that is what contributed to not feeling the need to go for a walk every day (and it felt safer, to me). Just to sit outside with a nice coffee, or spend time in the garden doing some of my writing and coaching work is so fab, listening to the birds singing, the sound of running water, breeze gently blowing (it's starting to sound like something out of a Julie Andrews film!).

It's not always enough though and there is no better thing than aerobic exercise to 'defog' your brain and get the blood pumping.

Recently as I mentioned I have been suffering physical ailments that have prevented me from getting stuck into anything too intense but we had bought a cross-trainer some time ago and I love making that part of my morning routine where possible. It's not too technical, it's very good for working the various muscle groups and if you have space (ours is kept/used in our converted cellar space) it's another great way to just add a little something into your day. I started with just 10 minutes 3 times a week, it doesn't sound like much at all but like everything, I always figure 10 minutes is better than nothing!

Another thing I started recently was using a mini-trampoline. Small enough to be easily moved around the house, and not so big as to get in everyone's way. I try to have at least a few minutes on this in the morning (but I don't do that every day either) to clear away the cobwebs and get me ready for the day ahead.

When I first joined a gym, back in 2011, to work on improving both my mental health and my physical fitness, I opted for one that would be no effort to get to. I had to pass it almost every day on my post office run so there was no excuse. Simply named '30 minute fitness' I loved that simple concept, it's known as circuit training, you make your way around a circuit of different equipment which in turn exercises and tones up every different muscle group in your body. The results for me were pretty astounding actually. I looked and felt fantastic and I always noticed it when I missed a day or a few days for whatever reason. It was right there in my mood dips! We all have them, it isn't always possible to identify or justify the reason but I have got better and better at that over the years.

Later on in my journey, I joined a spa & wellness gym, for an unbeatable price I had access to a gym, swimming, jacuzzi, sauna, steam room, you name it – it was perfect for winding down and relaxing (much needed in my single mum days) – to be honest I rarely used the gym facilities, it was the jacuzzi and pool I loved, but the eventual reason I had to cancel my membership was the distance to make the best use of all these wonderful things, taking me 25 minutes each way to drive there so became quite impractical as my life got busier.

I think that's been key to the wide variety of things I have tried over the years, as shared here. Just starting something and trying to make it part of a routine, without putting myself under too much pressure. No one needs to be so hard on themselves! All of these suggestions are just simple ideas to try and help you experiment with something that might help you find that balance you deserve.

Nothing in life can always be picture perfect though and I fully understand that you might be reading this thinking:

> *"What a load of twaddle, I feel crap enough about my life, I don't need some silly woman telling me airy-fairy 'just get outside and enjoy the fresh air' rubbish."*

These are honestly all things I have done in my life when things got tough, sometimes as a combination of efforts, often just one thing consistently has been enough.

If you have read my first book 'Onward and Upward', you will know I have endured more than my fair share of trials and tough times and come through them, I am still (very much) smiling and I did the majority of that without any kind of medical intervention at all. That is not to say how you are feeling isn't tough, everyone has their limits and we both know that's the reason you reached out for this book.

Whatever you do, if you find yourself in a dark place, please be sure to see your GP as soon as possible, it may be a chemical imbalance or medical condition that only prescription medication can help with, and I can't stress enough the importance of getting that properly investigated. Sometimes medical intervention is essential.

You are worth it!

PS: DON'T FORGET TO GRAB YOUR BONUS MATERIAL!

If you enjoyed the exercise at the end of the self-care section in chapter one, don't forget the bonus workbook I've created just for you!

Visit **bit.ly/YGTworkbook**

Where you can download your very own fully complimentary PDF workbook with simple exercises you can do to accompany each and every section of this book! They will help you get clear on what you need to do right now to better support yourself – and I'll be there cheering you on.

Food and your Mood

Don't be scared by the title of this chapter!

You might read it and think, oh hell, she's going to suggest I go vegan, or drop all the things I like to eat best and start eating grass-fed chicken every day.

Wrong!

What I will say, first of all, is 'you are what you eat'. By that, I definitely don't mean if you eat beef, you are a cow.

Just think about this sentence for a moment. 'If you eat crap, you will feel like crap'.

I definitely noticed a difference in my moods when I paid a bit more attention to what I consumed. However there is a lot more to this chapter than simply 'eat good, feel good' and I need to share that with you, a little later on.

The rate at which our body burns the wrong kind of energy is scary. If you fill yourself up with sugary food and drink, add sugar to your tea or coffee, drink fizzy pop all day, snack on processed foods, you are bound to notice some kind of 'afternoon slump'. There is a huge irony in me writing this at the moment, as I am all over the place with my eating habits, having recently postponed my wedding by a whole year, faced some tough life-altering decisions head-on, and dealing with daily 'lockdown' life of some sort or other – and I have no physical energy to do anything... there is no coincidence in this (my willpower has clearly been used up, for the moment).

When you feed your body with the proper fuel, you function a whole lot better.

There are a lot of ways to find out what works best for you.

You can do this intuitively, by observing, noticing a pattern in which food groups, such as dairy, wheat (I have chosen these two as they are common naughties) have either a positive or negative effect on you, and eliminating the baddies, boosting your immune system with more of the good stuff, starting with keeping a food diary. You may have noticed certain types of food, such as these perhaps that just don't 'do' you any good. Pay attention to this, it can be really helpful if you are struggling with your moods because they don't just affect your digestion or waistline.

You can manage this by eating certain food groups only at certain times of the day, or separate from other food groups – it's called 'Food combining'. I did this once many years ago, and it was life-changing. It actually brought me back from a severe problem with acid reflux which had me almost starving myself, because it affected me so much I became scared to eat at all. Before this, I'd had several years of watching different food group patterns in my son, when we changed a lot of fundamental things about his diet to improve his behaviour and coping mechanisms.

You can also change the way you think about food if you choose to by investigating something called the 'Blood type' diet. More than just a diet, this is a lifestyle choice and a complete eye-opener to how you do so many things in your life. Put quite simply, each and every person's blood group, from A to O, affects greatly how they absorb nutrients from and process the different food groups. Some of them shouldn't be ingested by those groups at all. It's an absolutely fascinating kind of diet to implement because it has you seeing so many different triggers you had previously not even considered.

As an example, I'm a Type O. This is the primeval, caveman blood type from many moons ago when man first came into existence (in whichever way you believe that came about). They hunted animals, did not use them for their milk, did not go digging around in the meadow for tasty grassy morsels, and basically just ate what they killed. Pulses weren't really a thing, and caffeine didn't exist back then. As such, the ideal food groups for a Type O are to eat meat, avoid dairy and caffeine and go back to the bare basics. The result of this for your body is that you will find you digest everything much more 'properly', your system is not slowed down by overworking, processing foods that weren't intended for your blood type, and you begin to thrive. It can be hard to begin with, getting used to it all (I went completely cold turkey on everything at once, which was mind-bending, but I'm an all or nothing kind of girl) but it is honestly a huge mindset shift that you won't regret. It's definitely worth investigating if you are starting to recognise what I have said as common triggers.

Now I'd like to talk about using a diet to support other conditions.

Not nearly enough people adopt an alternative approach through diet when trying to manage difficult behaviours in their children, in my opinion.

In 2002, my then 5year old was diagnosed with autism. It was a very difficult time, I went through a grieving process for the future that was never going to be, having already lost my 2nd child in 1996, my rainbow child now had a spectrum all of his own. I had just separated from his dad too, and my resolve was weak. His behaviour was just beyond exhausting. We dealt with a LOT of tantrums, trials, hair-raising moments, often related to inexplicable, seemingly (to us) unimportant things. I couldn't get into his head because it worked in such a different way to anything I had ever known. He would literally throw himself into people and things when it wasn't going his way, would reach out to passing traffic 'to see what it felt like', walking on spongey bricks in the path of oncoming traffic to experience something other than the pain-centred world he was beginning to know. (It's impossible to explain how as a parent you just see your child do these dangerous things and feel completely helpless, we felt like putting him in a straitjacket just to walk down the road!).

The thing about autism that you may not know is, their physiological makeup can be quite different. Often, the blood-brain barrier is incomplete, sometimes damaged, allowing toxins to pass through that should otherwise be filtered out and keep their system pure. They cannot break down the proteins from gluten and dairy in the same way as we do, instead, they find their way into the system in a toxic form – the technical term is gluteomorphine in the case of gluten or casomorphine in the case of dairy. In effect what happens is, they are walking around high on a kind of drug!

You may have noticed in your Autistic or Aspergers child if this is the case, that they don't seem to have much of a pain barrier, they bump and crash and it never seems to hurt?

When he was around 2 or 3, I took my son on a bus ride one day, and as we boarded the bus I noticed a damp patch on his head. He had cracked his head open and blood was streaming through his hair. Because he was absorbing a lot of these proteins at the time (it was a long time before diagnosis or even acknowledging his condition) he never felt a thing. As I write this I can't believe a mother could 'not' notice something like this, but life at the time was a daily challenge of epic proportions.

Maybe you have noticed they refuse a lot of food groups? Some of this is due to the sensations, the textures, as this is a common thing for them, but also it can be because of the effect of the gluteo or casomorphine numbing everything for them - so much that they just don't have those senses to appreciate the food right now. They associate food with being their 'fix' and only go for the groups that give them an instant hit.

Gluten can be found in many food groups, principally wheat, barley, oats, and rye, and casein in any animal-based dairy produce - including things like goats milk.

Now here's the thing. If you have looked into this further and made the decision to remove these from their diet, and it has been an issue for them, (this is often the only way to find out if it is, intolerance testing can be tricky and not all that accurate, or at least it wasn't in the UK when I did this in the mid-2000s) I just want to say one thing to you.

Buckle up buttercup, you are in for a bumpy ride.

Picture a drug addict whom you have removed the fix from. You've taken away their drugs and they want more, but have to go through a long, painful, very drawn-out withdrawal. It sounds horrid, and why would you want to put them (or you) through that? Just trust me when I say, if you do this right, it will be so worth it. We followed 5 years of this intensive type of diet therapy, and although we eventually made the decision to allow him to make his own choices, I am certain without a shadow of a doubt that those 5 years gave us the more manageable young adult that we have now than we otherwise would have had.

I met so many parents along the way who simply would say to me "you're very brave, I couldn't be doing with all that". But the way I saw it, stressful though it was, the alternative was already running everyone into the ground. The unmanageable, every day who what where when, continuous calls home from school, literally running around like a blue arsed fly as my dad would say, left me drained and no good to anyone. The option to invest time and money into improving his quality of life (and ours, let's be honest) was far better spent than sitting around twiddling my thumbs waiting for a cure or whatever.

We never touched things like Ritalin. Melatonin, yes, the sleep hormone which they are naturally lacking we used to have supplements of that, but not once in his childhood did we have him taking any kind of medication for his behaviour. I still don't know how we did that, his behaviour at school at times was *completely* off the chart. I remember the conversation with the school secretary early on 'But Miss Rogerson, he is just so difficult to deal with, how do you cope?' - I was at the end of my tether, the school couldn't deal with his behaviour and I really just wanted to scream 'WHO SAYS I'M COPING?!'.

It wasn't an easy undertaking though, not by any stretch, so please don't let me make you think I made it look like a walk in the park. Some days it was so far from that it isn't even funny. We went to hell and back doing this diet. His dad didn't always agree with my choices over it, and since we had separated by this time, finding a middle ground was tough, that would hamper our progress a lot of the time, but it HAD to be done. I battled everyone over it actually, the school, the family, my son (who just wanted to eat random things like shoes by this point)... you name it.

It gets way more complicated than this the further you look into it, but if you are considering something like this as an option, it's important to do your research. There have been books published about this as a topic by itself but science, availability of foods, etc can change quite dramatically so make sure you are reading up-to-date information. It's known as the GFCF diet, and if you start googling, you will find (like most things) many different opinions about it, but you can learn enough about the simplest approach to it, to help you decide if it's something you want to try.

The reason I chose to cover this particular diet in a 'self-help' book, is because it made a difference to all of us in the long run. I bought myself some sanity by undertaking this, so although it was about helping my son, in the long run, it also bought me some sanity. I made much more informed choices about his diet and it reflected on my own choices too. And I also fully believe that his teenage years, although they were tough, could have been so much tougher had we not at least attempted this.

That's the thing about change, we can look for one thing and find something else that happens as a result, a side effect – serendipity is a beautiful thing.

Keep your eyes on the prize!

PS: DON'T FORGET TO GRAB YOUR BONUS MATERIAL!

If you enjoyed the exercise at the end of the self-care section in chapter one, don't forget the bonus workbook I've created just for you!

Visit **bit.ly/YGTworkbook**

Where you can download your very own fully complimentary PDF workbook with simple exercises you can do to accompany each and every section of this book! They will help you get clear on what you *need* to do right now to better support yourself – and I'll be there cheering you on.

Counselling, Self help groups, Befriending

Let's talk.

Talking about things is so important. When we bottle things up, we don't only try to pretend they aren't happening, we also 'store' the energy associated with them, and all of this can have an impact for many years. While there are lots of ways to express yourself, a good old fashioned natter can't be overlooked. There are, however, many forms of talking therapy and I just wanted to take the time to tell you about what I have done and used over the years to begin to find my way forward.

Back in 1996 and 1997, I had my first experience of seeing a professionally trained counsellor. It was the darkest year of my life (and I've had a few tough ones), the stillbirth of my son Jay at full term, followed a few months later by a miscarriage at 11 weeks with the same words 'I can't find a heartbeat'.

I stopped feeling anything, I was numb. I hated that lack of feeling anything. Having spent some months in deep dark grief as a young mum with no baby to love, all of a sudden it was like my emotions had just been switched off, and it felt wrong to me, how could I possibly feel nothing after all that?

I had visits from my community midwife and our local GP was amazing, but they felt powerless to help, they had never known anything quite like what happened to me that year, so when we spoke again and I said I need help, I want to see someone, they agreed it was the best thing.

I started seeing my counsellor in late 1996, I would go every single week, pour my heart out to her, and she would listen. I would talk about how things were at home. If you've ever experienced the loss of a child, you will know that it can affect many couples in many different ways – you may grieve together initially, but then eventually life must go on, your partner or husband will have to go back to work, and you are just there, with empty arms. That was how it felt for me, although I had a 4-year-old also at home, my world had just come to a standstill. I don't think I parented him particularly well during this time, although he was always fed, clothed, and luckily being of nursery age meant he had some sort of outlet of his own – and he was a very happy child too.

My counsellor would help me to put things into perspective a little, I would often let off steam about things that had happened or been said to me during that time, I struggled with that a lot, people were so desperate to understand but I just felt like no one possibly could. The thing about a professionally trained counsellor, is they are not there to tell you what to do, how to feel, or give their opinion, but gently, they can encourage you to begin to find the way forward again, work out what you may be doing that isn't particularly beneficial to you, or find new things to help support you. I heavily relied on those sessions, and my 'Angel mummy' friends I had made, they cushioned me, they knew my pain, they never judged.

Finding a safe space to let everything out is SO important if you are struggling. No-one needs know you are having counselling if you don't want to share that with anyone, but there is honestly NO shame in it at all – it is encouraged now, more than ever, to be open about your struggles. That might not be something that comes naturally to you, and that's fine, don't worry about that, but if bottling things up is doing you no good, you need to find somewhere to let it out.

A trained counsellor is an excellent place to go for that when you have your regular spot. When you can at least try to save up all your hurts until 11am on a Thursday or whatever your regular slot is, and just let it all go. They will never leave you open, just walking out into the world as a sobbing wreck, they are trained to help you piece yourself together again and it is so valuable if you are in a time of turmoil. I know this was a concern for me, attempting to make a transition from feeling numb back to feeling sad all over again, I was scared of opening myself up and ever being able to stop the leaky tap that had become my eyes (I didn't wear eye make up for a very long time). I needed safety and security.

This brings me to talk about self-help groups.

There are groups out there now for all kinds of sharing.

I genuinely believe I may not have come through some of my darkest times without the regular outlet of the Bereaved Parents' support group which met every Thursday, run by 2 lovely health visitors who came to feel more like family. I wouldn't have known this place even existed had I not started moving in those circles, and something like that might be just what you need, right now, and thanks to the power of the internet, much easier to find. I went week after week, month after month, and wouldn't miss it for anything, even during school holiday time. It became my one constant.

To be able to talk in a group with other parents, more often than not they were mums - but not always, and the health professionals responsible for running the group would hold us all in the safe space during our 90 minute (ish) sessions, with a welcome cup of coffee, and help us when we were hurting the most, feeling raw and as if no-one understood our suffering.

The pain of losing a child is like no other. All your hopes and dreams are gone, sometimes in a heartbeat. Your world is changed beyond all recognition, forever, and if you are surrounded by people who try to say they know how you feel because they lost their dog/they lost their mum/they failed their driving test (trust me, I have heard it ALL over the years…) you will find yourself feeling lost and misunderstood. Your heartache can feel diminished, making you question if you are making a fuss over nothing - this is how it felt for me, anyway.

I would never say my pain is worse than someone else's because, in the 25 years since I delivered my son into the world, only to have him taken away without even opening his eyes, I have found a place of understanding that we each write our own story, walk our own path and comparison of others' pain for me was so detrimental when I was just trying to get through the days. Maybe that sounds harsh, but all I know is that some of the comparisons made when I was struggling to find a reason to get up every single day, often held me in a place of not understanding why it hurt so bloody much if others were suffering too.

The bereaved parents I met along the way, they were different. Fondly nicknamed 'the group no one wants to belong to', between myself and a solid group of also bereaved mums, over many years we have helped each other through some exasperating times following the loss of our children.

There are, of course, many charities that exist that are there for specific kinds of loss – SANDS, Compassionate Friends, Families of murder victims – to be honest, the wide range of different groups is possibly a bit overwhelming if you think too hard – but it is more than likely there will be one that best fits your kind of loss if that is something you need right now. You are not alone.

The relevant ones to my story can be found in the useful links section in the back of this book.

Befriending.

What is befriending?

When you befriend, you are offering support to someone who needs to know they can reach out when things get tough, to listen, and hold space for them without judgement.

If you have ever been befriended by anyone or reached out to someone who needs it, you will know the strange comfort it gives you.

The first time I ever befriended anyone I think I was in 3rd year juniors! I was hand-picked to offer an understanding ear to a young lad who was due to go into a new class with a teacher who had something of a reputation for being quite harsh. The reason I was chosen? I had a unique rapport with said teacher having spent more time than most in the classroom in the previous year when I had an ankle injury that left me on crutches for several weeks. She wasn't all that scary and it was thought by the staff that I could offer an understanding ear to this young lad who had no idea what to expect from being in her class. I honestly never understood it at the time, or for some years, but I know now that was my empathetic heartstrings being plucked and it was going to be something I would always be known for – an understanding ear, and a damn good listener!

My next and deepest experience of befriending was the kind you can never, ever teach. During my time volunteering for SANDS, I spent some 3 or more years as a befriender to bereaved parents, usually after having lost their child to stillbirth or neonatal death (death in the first 4 weeks of life). Having experienced it first hand myself, I had the exact skill set needed, but my god it was tough!

The first call came – I will never forget it – when my rainbow child, my 3rd born son who came after those dark days of 1996, was celebrating his 1st birthday. We had a bit of a houseful, some tiny playmates and their very special mums had all come round for a birthday tea. There was an amazing feeling of wow, he IS here, and we made it through his first year! So when the phone rang I was in exceptionally good spirits.

To pick up the phone not expecting that devastating sadness at the other end was just, well I can't explain it. It was almost silent, the heartbroken mum at the end of the line stumbled over her words, eventually managing to tell me that she had lost not 1 but 3 children, her stillborn triplets. My heart was breaking for her that day – all I could do was listen. Whatever I said at this moment wouldn't change how she felt, but I was with her, right there in that call. Because I know exactly how it feels to be the devastated mum finding it in me somehow to pick up the phone and call what was in effect a total stranger. I would just gently coax her that whatever she wanted to say, or not say, was okay. If she just wanted to cry down the phone, that was okay too. I would just 'be there'.

The toughest thing about grief is that feeling of it being never-ending. It never goes away completely. As I sit here writing this, some 22 years after I took that first call, and 25 years since my second child Jay was stillborn, the day after he was due, I have never forgotten the first time I picked up the phone to find someone who could listen without trying to have any clever answers.

Because there aren't any.

Heartbroken mums – or parents, grandparents, siblings – will never truly know the answer to their 'why'? I spent months and months just repeating the same things over and over again, it was the most indescribable* feeling and I would get so frustrated with myself. When I found my befriender, someone who had experienced something almost identical to me – a rare occurrence indeed – I clung to her with everything I could find. I didn't feel I belonged anywhere otherwise. That feeling of belonging when you can lean on someone – often someone who is still on their own journey in some way, but usually a bit further down the road than you – you can't learn that anywhere, it can only be experienced.

So if your journey is one that you know needed a special someone you could always go to, no matter how dark the days ahead seemed, perhaps this is something you could find some comfort in. That alone probably sounds a bit odd – how can you find comfort in being reminded of a difficult place you couldn't see the way out of? How would you have found the way out without that person, would probably be the question you could ask yourself.

There are plenty of befriender training workshops all over the country, often more specific to the type of help you are wanting to offer. Many of the charities such as Cruse, SANDS, and other support networks (because of course, it doesn't have to be befriending for grief, there are many difficult situations in life where you need to know you can call on someone) should usually have these resources available for you to access them and see how or if you can help someone in need.

As difficult as it was, I am so thankful I once had this available to me, I truly don't know how I would have found the way through my darkest days without it.

*I have starred this word, because for over 25 years I have tried and tried to find a word awful enough to describe the heartbroken feeling, and there simply isn't one. No matter how many words in the English language, no one word can cover it.

Relationship counselling - a different kind of counselling.

One of the toughest journeys of my more recent years was finding my way through to the end of my first marriage. It took a long time to travel that path, but throughout I knew I wanted to one day be able to say 'I gave it my all'.

It's a bit scary to think how close that came to the raw truth of not having anything left to get up and face the day, on some occasions. Having the courage to keep going when you're not always sure exactly why you are doing that, or what you are doing it for, can be emotionally exhausting and for some months I teetered on a very fine line. It definitely felt more like I was just existing.

We had come to a cross-roads and I felt it wasn't just my words he needed to hear any more. I wanted apologies, I wanted accountability, I needed honesty on both sides. I thought that perhaps the traditional 'marriage guidance' counselling might help me find my way with some of that. We had already tried everything else, we weren't even living under the same roof anymore.

We went on a waiting list – it wasn't all that long, but when the brief introductory session began with our female counsellor, a lady in her senior years, I knew it was going to be tough. Because there had been abuse and subsequently police involvement in the later stage of our relationship, we had first of all to undergo a risk assessment, each of us independently of the other - it wasn't like we were even starting it as a couple, to begin with.

If you are ever in this position, I ask you to please be honest from day one – with yourself. After this somewhat degrading experience of having to go into detail about what happened, how we felt about the issues raised, we slowly began to talk about what it was we wanted to achieve from the sessions. I will be honest now and say I don't think I ever felt I was completely able to speak my truth in front of my husband at the time. I felt that after the session was over things would start to get picked apart and we would be reliving the same discussions over and over again. I didn't have the energy for that. Or the desire to keep doing it, to be honest. My feeling was, in that room, he would say what he felt was expected, and that too in a counselling setting can make things seem different to how they are in reality. The thing was, these sessions weren't cheap. But I felt there were many more layers to unpick than we managed in the sessions we had. After a few sessions, we started to feel as though things were a little more in sync (no doubt helped by the fact that we were still living apart, I think that took the pressure off immensely) and we managed a family holiday where I found we got along much better than I could remember for a long time, things just happened and we all enjoyed the time we spent together.

Unfortunately for us, this wasn't sustainable in the real world. It felt as though we were living some kind of 'fantasy' life, where we had fallen out, got back on track, and would live our lives just as we were – yet I still carried the can as a single mum, taking care of my sons, running my business, keeping a roof over our heads, paying all the bills and battling a huge debt - not of my own doing. It felt as though I was 2 people living 2 different lives. Not good for my mental health, as I would come to discover.

That is not to say it can't be more successful for other people. I have seen relationships come back from the brink after some time apart - I admire them, truly I do. I do feel that I have quite high expectations of what 'normality' should feel like and that can be hard to live up to, especially for someone who doesn't appreciate it.

If you are going to go down a road such as this one, I think it's important you are crystal clear that it truly is what you want, to work on a common goal together. It may be that it helps you both to work out that perhaps your relationship isn't for you anymore. And if that's the right decision, it's okay – it will be okay. There are no cast-iron guarantees in this world and when you are talking about the happiness of yourself and your family it's important to find that balance. You have to know that whatever the outcome, a healthier approach is always going to feel better in the long run than just not bothering anymore. It will help you to find whatever closure it is that you seek.

Whew!

I have covered a lot of ground here, and your head might be spinning a little. If, after reading this you have no idea which, if any of these options are for you, just take a minute to think about what feels good. What would give you the most comfortable outcome at the moment?

You don't want to feel like this forever - forever is a long time anyway.

Take one small step toward the thing that feels like maybe it could make a difference, and start there.

You can do this, I believe in you.

PS: DON'T FORGET TO GRAB YOUR BONUS MATERIAL!

If you enjoyed the exercise at the end of the self-care section in chapter one, don't forget the bonus workbook I've created just for you!

Visit **bit.ly/YGTworkbook**

Where you can download your very own fully complimentary PDF workbook with simple exercises you can do to accompany each and every section of this book! They will help you get clear on what you *need* to do right now to better support yourself – and I'll be there cheering you on.

Diaries and Journaling

Have you ever had that one person you could tell anything to, confide in, without judgement or debate?

Since I was a young girl, probably in my early teens, I have always kept a diary. I remember the very first one my Gran bought for me, it was a pretty, floral thing with a lock and key, It was one of those undated 5-year things and I remember starting it thinking, yeah right, I will never reach the last pages of this... Little did I know by the time I had finished the final page, many years later, I would be a completely different person.

My Gran was a writer too, she understood my tendency to express myself best in words. The opening page of my first book, *Onward and Upward,* is dedicated to this wonderful woman and my son, Jay, and the first line begins with a diary excerpt from when I was just 16 years old.

I've always found it the easiest way to keep a clear and open mind. Just 'brain-dumping' all my thoughts and innermost feelings onto a page where no one ever needs see them, judge them, or as I thought, mock me for them. They were my private thoughts and belonged to me, yet I still wrote as if one day they might be found, perhaps even read by someone else. Strange, I know.

I used to write things like 'I'm so glad I have been able to say this to you, you never answer back' and it was true. I am certain it saved me from dipping more often into depression which I had a mild tendency for, as one of life's over-thinkers, even before I hit more difficult times later on.

When I kept my diaries as a young girl, I always knew I could confide in my diary. There was never going to be an issue of trust and I shared my deepest, darkest secrets just between me and my book. I never realised of course at the time that I would come to look back on it almost 30 years later and draw from those experiences to share memories exactly as they happened when I became a published author in 2018.

Excerpts from my diaries spanning 1990 to the present day (2021) include pivotal events in my life (there are many), including:

- My first love, and the teenage pregnancy which followed shortly after.
- Leaving home aged 18 and moving to a strange city far away from my friends and family.
- The stillbirth of my 2nd child when I was just 20 years old, and the subsequent pregnancies that followed.
- Slipping in and out of depression (although I know I didn't realise it at the time).
- Emotions around milestones of my children growing up.
- The unspoken grief following the diagnosis of autism in my 5-year-old.
- A long term relationship breakdown, followed by the complexities of a new relationship and attempting to blend my new family life.
- The trials of being a small business owner.
- Supporting a partner with a chronic health condition, the complications in my married life, and its' eventual breakdown.
- Emotional and psychological abuse.
- Finding myself and my recovery from a toxic relationship.
- Learning what it truly means to love someone after I met the love of my life and began a brand new, real-life happy ever after.
- The gruelling long-term effects of our divorces and battles over access

and custody.
- Planning and then postponing my second wedding.
- Living through a global pandemic.

Yikes! Looking at that, it could be a book all by itself (did I mention *Onward and Upward*? I have covered much of my journey in there, it's not as exhausting a read as that list would have you believe, it's been done in a very uplifting, forward-looking way as the title suggests, but at the same time is very real, raw and relatable). As you can see, the experiences I have drawn from are many and varied, and the fact that I am still standing, to be here writing this book so I can help you, means I know my stuff.

Keeping a diary during these exceptionally difficult times was so beneficial to me, and I felt it saved me on many an occasion. I would pick them up and re-read them weeks, sometimes months later, and could see how far I had come. They were good for reminding me how lucky I was to have the wonderful people who have made it into my life, they would also serve to remind me of some of the mistakes I had made and help me to truly learn the lessons I believe they were sent for.

If this isn't something you have tried, or you didn't realise perhaps just how beneficial it could be for you, check out this section in the *Bonus Materials workbook* (link at the end of each chapter).

Journaling

Now I would just like to say something here about keeping a diary, and journaling.

They are quite different things. I am still very much honing the craft of journaling, as it is so different from the way I usually do things.

Keeping a diary can serve you in exactly the way I have detailed above. It is about recording your thoughts and feelings in that moment, whether to preserve them, to look back on in future years, or to clear some grey matter in your mind to allow you to think more clearly. Think of it like 'defragging' your own personal hard drive. That is how it has always felt to me.

Journaling is a very specific way of processing your journey. When journaling, you go inward, sitting quietly, ask yourself a question, examine the whys and wherefores, sometimes many times over until you find the answer that was probably there all along. You tune into your intuition, that inner voice until you uncover what it is you want the answer to. We all have this ability, I feel I have much work to do to fully get to grips with how powerful it can be, but I am not ashamed to say exactly that.

As I write this chapter, I am in a place of changing direction in my life. I have decided during recent months to close the doors on a full-time business I have grafted on for many years, and start again, on a different path. It is bloody scary, I am still figuring out exactly what that path is, but I do know that journaling will help me find some of those answers.

There is no doubt in my mind that Covid-19 has had a part to play in my decision to change direction. All around the world people are reassessing their lives, their choices, their priorities, and many are deciding to choose again. It's okay to do exactly that, especially when you feel, as I have experienced on many occasions, that your world has turned upside down – life is too short!

When you decide to change something in your world, no matter what it is, journaling it out can help you find the most natural way forward. Tuning into your inner voice, what your heart truly wants, is an art form envied by many, and when you are heart-led your life can become much easier, and calmer. You can surrender to the path you are meant to follow, and it is often something you are naturally gifted in.

I'd love to know if you already have a feeling you know what your path is?

Me? I have always loved books and writing. Always.

As detailed above, they featured highly in my life from quite a young age (it was years before the diary thing started up – I can still picture myself stood at the front of the class in junior school insisting to our teacher that I be allowed to read out the short story I had written, she never asked me to write it but I wanted to share it with the class, and yes, I did get my way – got a gold star too as a matter of fact!).

Over the years, I have kept my diary, dipped in and out of many books, read some fascinating real life and fiction books, and always loved the escape they provide. I think I always dreamed I would be known for writing fiction, to be honest. But that is beside the point (maybe one day). Sometimes years have passed where either life was too busy or it didn't occur to me that I should write about what was happening in my life. Writing has always been there, but I just haven't paid as much attention to it.

As I have said in recent months there has been more time to think about things and address what we want from the future. When I sat down and wrote about doing what I love, it didn't involve actually doing what I was doing in my business, I sort of fell into that once upon a very long time ago and it has just evolved and kept evolving from there. I learned a lot along the way, honed many different skills, but ultimately it wasn't firing me up anymore.

WHAT HAS THIS GOT TO DO WITH JOURNALING I hear you ask?

It's all related – when you revisit something over and over again, whether it be in one sitting over a few cups of your favourite hot/cold drink, you can't stop thinking about it, or you feel like it's your chosen path, then it's time to get stuck in! If I hadn't started that filtering process – well quite simply, you wouldn't be sitting here reading this book. I knew from the end of my first book that other books were going to follow, I didn't know it was going to take quite so long, but life has been kinda busy – and I didn't listen to that inner voice telling me what I already knew.

So if you are stuck – maybe you are stuck in a job that doesn't light you up? Or dare I say it may be something else in your life right now just sucks, perhaps you are stuck in a relationship – trust me, I get it. Whatever it is, take some time, MAKE some time, to begin to work through it by yourself. No-one needs to know you're even doing it if you don't want them to.

And if it feels like the end of the world as you come to terms with some tough stuff, you can start again – you can always start again, even if it doesn't feel like it right now.

I want you to believe that – believe in yourself.

You've got this!

PS: DON'T FORGET TO GRAB YOUR BONUS MATERIAL!

If you enjoyed the exercise at the end of the self-care section in chapter one, don't forget the bonus workbook I've created just for you!

Visit **bit.ly/YGTworkbook**

Where you can download your very own fully complimentary PDF workbook with simple exercises you can do to accompany each and every section of this book! They will help you get clear on what you *need* to do right now to better support yourself – and I'll be there cheering you on.

The power of Letter writing

You can't beat proper handwritten letters.

Something I have always enjoyed ever since I was young is writing a letter. I must admit, it isn't something I have done so much of in more recent years, with the introduction of emails, but you really can't beat a good old fashioned letter. Even an email with the same intention can be just as powerful, and therapeutic too.

Letters have featured highly in my life for a very long time, from being wooed by my first proper boyfriend, where we spent weeks getting to know each other before we talked properly face to face, to the incredible letter I received from Mother Teresa shortly after the birth of my first child, when I was just 16, to keeping in touch with my family and friends when I left home aged just 18 – that was before the introduction of emails, and I wouldn't have been without them. I used to love receiving those letters, more often than not they lifted me in a way I couldn't understand.

Words can truly be that powerful!

I'd love to tell you the different ways I have used these to my advantage. Don't ever underestimate the catharsis behind writing something out, even if you have no intention of sending it to the recipient. I've had some of my best one-sided conversations in letters I never sent. It does help to get things in order, in your head, you don't have to worry that this person will be offended, upset, hurt or even have to worry about their response if you have no intention of sending it.

But sometimes you have that light bulb moment where you see from a different perspective, understand your feelings better, or maybe you just think, you know what, maybe I will just send it anyway. You can find the greatest insights in those moments.

I think this is the difference between emails and written letters – it's the timing. Emails can too easily be written in the heat of the moment and sent before you have the chance to think about what it is you are saying - there is always the 'draft' option! Conversely, in the days when letters were a much more featured form of communication, things were considered a lot more first – I really do think that - it could take anything from 2 to 5 days to reach your recipient, and if written in the heat of the moment that could easily have cooled off by then.

A lovingly written hand-addressed letter just has something about it, don't you think?

Throughout my most difficult times, I have felt so weighed down by the actions or insensitivities of others, or their responses to my burdens, and I haven't been able to find a way to express it in spoken form.

Leaving home aged 18, I found it very difficult to communicate well with my mum. My partner at the time wasn't a fan of the 'phone and I felt so isolated. When calls home did happen, I would always be worrying about how everyone else was and so never felt fully present in a conversation. In those early days, tempers sometimes ran high, getting things off my chest proved difficult to do on long-distance calls where you couldn't just talk things through and have a nice hug afterward, and I think I became quite withdrawn as a result.

On the odd occasion, I would write a letter to her. I didn't always send them, and I was really struggling but clearly in denial about how difficult I was finding things. I needed to get some clarity on my emotions. I felt so alone, and writing letters directed somewhere reminded me that I still had a connection with the outside world. It's hard to explain but I have always found it easier to express myself in written form, whatever that takes than I do by voicing things. I wouldn't say I was the silent type but I struggle with difficult conversations and confrontation, for sure. I find it's easier to process and work through your words in exactly the way you want to say them, but for those who don't communicate in quite the same way, it can come across as cold and unfeeling, cowardly even, just because you don't face them.

The simple fact is we are all different.

Some people can think more clearly when they aren't constantly trying to work with the latest responses before they've said what they want to say. Some of this might be coloured by the experience of being in relationships where you are too easily convinced that your opinions don't matter or are insignificant/irrelevant. I have learned a lot by navigating my way through these complex, sometimes toxic situations and owning it as my strength.

Sometimes it can make a world of difference just getting those thoughts out of your own mind, whether you direct them to the person in question or not.

One of my favourite things to do, particularly in our early days of going out, was to write letters to my now fiancé (still my fiancé, 2 years after the proposal. Thanks Covid!) while he was at work. We have such a strong energetic connection and I would miss him terribly. Sometimes I would just write how I was feeling, other times there might be something we were in the middle of understanding for our journey and I needed to process it in my own way. It would lighten the load on my mind and allow me to go about the other things I needed to do.

Those first months, in fact well over a year were incredibly intense and I found it very hard to concentrate on anything because our energies were so intensely bound to each other (it's a feeling that is incredibly hard to describe if you've never experienced it). Both of us being introverts we would easily be affected by the other one's energy, especially while dealing with emotionally stressful situations and we have certainly had our share of those in the time we have been together.

Anyway, I digress a little.

Another precious reason I found for letter writing was during the time of bereavement. When I lost my 2nd son, I was just 20 years old, he was due to be born when he sadly slipped away shortly before birth, for many months, and on all the anniversaries of his death for some years, I would write him a letter. I talked a lot about how I was feeling, I would tell him all the things that had happened in the time since my previous letter, just as if I could talk to him, and it brought me a great deal of comfort. On his first anniversary, I used the art of calligraphy to write out all the early letters by hand and kept them in a box alongside other mementoes. I cannot really describe how this comforted me, I had never experienced a loss like it, nor had anyone in my closest family. I felt so alone, and writing to him brought me closer to him, if only for a short while. I didn't know how to get through it, I simply followed my instincts, and somehow I made it through. I would also write letters at that time (still long before the invention of email) to my close friends, to both our mums, to my wonderful gran who was also a letter writer, and having that contact somehow kept me going (although I know I felt for a long while that it was touch and go).

If you haven't ever been a letter writer, that doesn't matter at all. Much like journaling and keeping a diary, you can remind yourself that it is for your own benefit, at least initially. You may have someone you are bumping up against constantly – maybe it is your partner, or perhaps one of your children or parents, or someone outside of your family.

Some years ago, I was going through a bit of a tough time with my eldest, during his teens, and he went to stay at his dad's. It was a really difficult time, I felt totally wretched as a mum I sat down and wrote him a heartfelt letter - I needed him to know I still loved him and why we concluded this was the best option, and how I could possibly imagine us moving forward from this horrible time. Whether it was his mature approach or the effect of what I said in a letter to I wrote to him, I don't know, but we started to pick away at the issues around the conflict and attempted to learn something from it. Talking hasn't often been the strong point of my sons, they are 21st century people for the most part but when required they usually manage to find words and open up the communication once more. We took very slow, very small steps back to our former home life, and thankfully, gradually settled back down again.

I like to think that my encouragement of being open to communicating had something to do with this but of course that can almost always depend on the attitude of the other person or people involved. Some people are just not good at sharing how they feel.

When you first pick up pen and paper to attempt this, you will probably feel very silly, worrying what others will think of what you have to say or how you say it. Don't worry about that. Focus on how it will make you feel to get those thoughts out of your head.

Whether you are in a struggling relationship and can't find a way forward - there is always a way. Maybe you are in a relationship with someone new but have 'old stuff' holding you back - a common theme I've noticed - write about that. Writing really can be so good for your mental health but also when directed at a recipient, it will lighten your mind, removing you from the situation a little, and even if never sent, you know that you perceive how the situation is making you feel.

It can help you open up a level of understanding you might otherwise find difficult to achieve. You can imagine yourself in a conversation with whoever it may be, without laying any of your problems out there until you have got to grips with them yourself. Maybe it will take more than that, you can always run it by a third party (someone neutral is the best idea if you do decide to try this approach) and ask for their honest opinion. Just get it all out of your head, how you feel, what it is that made you feel this way, how it perhaps could have been more sensitively put, an approach you might have preferred. In a long term relationship with your significant other, or someone who is to feature in your life for the foreseeable future, this is very important because it helps them to understand what makes you tick, how you operate, and if you don't offer them an insight to that understanding, they could just keep making the same mistakes. Don't expect people to mind read.

You can do anything you set your mind to – give it a try.

PS: DON'T FORGET TO GRAB YOUR BONUS MATERIAL!

If you enjoyed the exercise at the end of the self-care section in chapter one, don't forget the bonus workbook I've created just for you!

Visit **bit.ly/YGTworkbook**

Where you can download your very own fully complimentary PDF workbook with simple exercises you can do to accompany each and every section of this book! They will help you get clear on what you need to do right now to better support yourself – and I'll be there cheering you on.

Do it like no-one cares

No-one cares if you can't sing or dance! Do it anyway.

I started January 2016 with renewed hope, after a very tough year having separated from my husband, father to my 9-year-old. At this point, none of my sons had made it to the age of 10 before their parents split and I felt pretty crap about that. We were working on things and I was hopeful that 2016 was going to be the year when we figured it all out.

I really wanted to learn to sing! I liked the idea of having lessons, had no idea how much it might cost, or when on earth I was supposed to fit it in, as my family life was split across 2 homes, I was running my business while supporting my sons by myself financially. I was pretty tired but I still wanted to find the energy for me! It was early January when, having had this idea but done nothing about it, a Facebook post from one of my networking friends jumped off the screen at me.

'Sing like no-one's listening. Join us at West Bridgford on January 14th for the launch night of our Tuneless Choir, where you can sing just for fun, without worrying what you sound like'.

This sounded PERFECT for me at that moment. When I was in junior school, 2 of my closest friends were in the Sunday school choir and I always had that feeling of not being good enough to sing along with them when we used to belt out True Blue sat around our conjoined school desks. I still did but was always very self-conscious. So maybe I couldn't sing, but if this tuneless thing was right, it wouldn't matter and I could just have a go anyway.

January 14th felt like the most impossible date for me and I struggled up until the day itself trying to decide if I would go or stay home and be sad. It was the 20th birthday of my second son Jay, who had been stillborn at full term. What if I didn't feel like being happy that day? It comes around every year and I never know how I will feel on the day, unable to celebrate, just remember him quietly, light a candle, miss him more than the rest of the year, and not really want to see anyone in particular. Singing has always been one of those things to set me off if I'm feeling emotional, what if a song makes me cry that night and I won't know anyone, no-one will understand. Just like in so many years previously, I'll be remembered as 'the woman who always cries'.

I made a decision. If I feel like it on the day, I'm going. If I feel up to it, it will be the perfect way to honour my son – doing something good for ME, to comfort me and remind me after all this time that my life wasn't completely over when he died, that I found ways to be alive I had never once imagined possible. Maybe it would even cheer me up on one of those sad days.

I wouldn't regret a moment of this decision, it was the best thing I could have done for myself in that moment. The songlist was MADE for me – Bon Jovi was first on the list, there was some Abba, bit of Wham, it sent excited shivers through me. I saw one or two familiar faces, Nadine in particular who was the person responsible for the whole thing, as well as another lovely networking friend who, as it happened, didn't know anyone else either, so we sat together at the back of the church. It was really busy! It seemed as though a lot of people loved the idea of singing for fun, and I felt so proud in that moment – proud of myself, for being brave enough to go for it, and proud that I had followed my instincts and embraced the opportunity the second I spotted the Facebook post. We all had so much fun that evening, I will be honest, we didn't sound great, but that wasn't the point of the exercise.

Singing for any reason is so good for your mental health, but when you are completely carefree in any activity and let go of your inhibitions, there is an added bonus - the endorphins flow (just like if you are into extreme sports or anything else that releases the happy hormone serotonin) - that you don't even have to concentrate on what you are doing particularly. Everyone who showed up just seemed so happy to be there, it was brilliant.

My personal journey with West Bridgford Tuneless Choir - who define being tuneless as "lacking the ability, practice or confidence to sing in tune" was to become fundamental to my mental health during that year (and ones that followed, but in particular 2016) as it fast became my non-negotiable. If I did nothing else for myself I would make sure I could get to sing at choir twice a month, and as the year progressed that was how I got through some *really* tough stuff.

We had a lot of time at home that year where my sons couldn't be left alone together, after a harrowing incident which caused us all so much anxiety, so I really had to pull out all the stops to be able to continue singing. The problem I found was that as the person responsible for babysitting (my then-husband, who no longer lived with us) was also the person to undo all the hard work I had done on 'me', almost instantly, pretty much every time I returned home from a choir session. As if I 'shouldn't' be making anything about myself a priority. So I found myself on this rollercoaster and knew there was no way I could give up on this all-important piece of the puzzle.

As that year progressed, and my marriage crumbled a little more, slowly but surely it became harder and harder to make it all work. My last singing 'engagement' for some time was to be a performance in the local high school. I felt so great after that, we were all buzzing, yet somehow the conversation that followed had started the 'penny drop'. It wasn't 'just' the stuff I was dealing with, with my sons that had me struggling – I was facing an impossible decision, how could I see a future with someone who didn't seem to like to see me lifting this huge cloud (almost single-handed), prioritising my mental health or even being remotely happy for a brief time?

I stepped back from my involvement with the choir for a while, so I could sort my life out. Luckily, it was during this time that my self-care routine became a priority and I found additional things I could do, that didn't cost any money, but helped me somehow stay afloat while it was finally concluded that our marriage had no future and life was set to change big time – for the better, at long last.

I followed what the choir had been up to at this time, and I got serious FOMO (fear of missing out) but loved seeing how much fun they were having. One day, that would be me again, I hoped.

It was July 2017 when, after a lot of inner work, focusing on my own happiness, I met the love of my life, my soulmate Bruce. Early on, we had numerous conversations about our love of music, he loved karaoke, and although I had never tried it I knew that with my singing brain in gear I would easily get up and perform in front of people now, whether they wanted to listen or not! By September, we were really finding our feet as a couple and so it was time to get back to choir, this time with a singing partner in crime.

We are fondly known by all as 'The Tuneless Lovebirds' – especially because it was at our choir, one evening in February 2019 when Bruce orchestrated, with our choir leaders' help, getting down on one knee in front of everyone (probably over 100 people) and asking me to marry him! I never expected that, it was absolutely magical. The video is available on youtube if you fancy a peek, still makes me cry every time I watch it.

My tuneless journey doesn't stop there – if you go on to read the Law of Attraction chapter, I talk about how I came to be appointed the Manager of West Bridgford Tuneless Choir in late 2020 – having now had the first couple of sessions as manager, we have many happy members who are all so supportive, it means they get to carry on singing and Nadine can see out another dream and enjoy her escape to the country! I am so thrilled to be able to say that I have landed this job, I love singing with the choir so much, it does me so much good, I sing for fun and now I can get paid for it too! Marvellous.

When you take on the 'doing like no one's listening/ watching', you will find yourself applying it to so many other things.

Ever been to a silent disco?

There's a really simple way you can do this without it costing you a penny.

Load up a playlist of songs that really get you moving – I LOVE 80s music and could happily dance to it for hours, so I would probably go for that, but whatever works best for you is something that gets you moving. Just pop on your headphones, choose a time when you are least likely to be disturbed, and just really go for it! You can move and jig like no one's watching (and maybe they aren't), without a care in the world for if it looks a little bit (lot) unchoreographed, the point of the exercise is really just to get you moving, lift your spirits, raise your vibration to boost your mood. The more you focus on these things you enjoy, the better you will feel in yourself.

And guess what?

The better you feel in yourself, the easier other things in your life will become – even though you will still be presented with challenges along the way, they will feel more bearable. I can honestly say that, because in the past year I have bounced back SO much faster from the challenges of 2020 (and we had a fair few personal challenges of our own at the time too) so even as I write this during Lockdown 3, I am upbeat, positive, focused and happy.

Anything is possible - if you believe it is.

PS: DON'T FORGET TO GRAB YOUR BONUS MATERIAL!

If you enjoyed the exercise at the end of the self-care section in chapter one, don't forget the bonus workbook I've created just for you!

Visit **bit.ly/YGTworkbook**

Where you can download your very own fully complimentary PDF workbook with simple exercises you can do to accompany each and every section of this book! They will help you get clear on what you *need* to do right now to better support yourself – and I'll be there cheering you on.

Creative pursuits and Hobbies

Over the years

I have tried many and varied 'hobbies/creative pursuits' in search of some kind of peace. I think that's what it was for anyway. I don't think I ever consciously decided to try something to calm me down, I always felt guided to them, even as a young girl I was always up to something creative – it was absolutely a mindful way of focusing my attention, whether intended or not. I thought it would be good to share some of these, what purpose they served me, and maybe it will give you some ideas of your own.

Knitting

When I was 16, as I may have mentioned, I became pregnant with my first child. Guided by both my sister and my boyfriend's mum, I learned to knit. It started with the small, such as a pair of baby bootees (and of course, being me, they weren't plain white. I never went for the obvious choices) with matching mittens. I don't think my son ever wore these when he came along but I was proud of them. It was something I used to sit and do for hours while chatting over a cuppa and getting to know my boyfriend's mum during a particularly emotional time of our lives, my first grandchild and her first grandchild. I gave birth in the middle of studying my A levels, which weren't particularly a form of escape for me, I think they stressed me out more than having a baby at such a young age. My mind was very foggy (most likely hormonal, I realise that now), I remember so well trying to concentrate on my studies and just not feeling like I was able to think, at all. But sitting down of an evening and picking up that knitting pattern, learning how to do a 'knit one, slip one, pass slipped stitch over' or a more complicated cable stitch felt like such an achievement. Of course, I made many mistakes along the way, but having the desired little jumpers and matching trousers slowly taking shape brought me such a rewarding buzz. It was the early 90s, baby clothes in any colour other than pastels were hard to come by so I made it my mission to dress our son in lovely brightly coloured clothes as much as possible, and on occasion, this meant they had to be made, and so I knew they were also unique – again another thing of mine, I never wanted to be the same as everyone else. It's just who I am.

Learning how to knit from scratch while my life was undergoing such a massive change, of becoming a mother, gave me something I couldn't have learned in a book. I think I probably knew that my entire life didn't 'just' have to revolve around being a mum (years later I would be woken up to the fact that being a mum was an incredible gift not everyone is graced with) but I could have something just for me too. I know that during this time I was battling with depression which I never owned up to, and so the creative hobbies were certainly something I was lucky to have found.

Jewellery making

We had just left home as young adults with a baby, our own little family. I lived far from home, miles away from everything I knew, and my partner then was at university full time. I had a baby to 'keep me company', but he wasn't talking sentences just yet and I got very lonely (so much so that I used to look forward to my visits to the local supermarket where one of the staff there was always chatting away to us). On one of our visits to town shopping, with parents visiting, I was treated to a jewellery making kit, which contained all I needed to make a few pairs of earrings. It wasn't something I had ever tried, but I liked the look of the kit. We had no money back then, so I was never able to treat myself to things like this, they were a luxury. I can picture it now.

Housework was not something I enjoyed, and having a small child and a house to run all of a sudden was a massive shock to the system. So I didn't bother. There would be toys strewn everywhere, dirty washing piling up, dishes in the sink from 2, maybe 3 days ago. I was always tired and the hours and days would pass and I would wonder why I didn't manage to get the house straight this week. This week merged into next week. Looking back, I was clearly depressed, but I never spoke to anyone about it. Yet I can still picture myself with saucers full of beads and jewellery findings, balanced on the plates from yesterday's lunch, tucked away in the corner of our pokey little living room just trying to escape long enough to make something pretty. I am not recommending you try it this way, even for a moment, it will drive you up the wall. I was desperate to make something that made me feel good, I think that's what it was about. I enjoyed making the earrings, combining the beautiful colours into something lovely while my toddler sat amid a floor filled with far too many toys, watching sesame street and paying no attention to any of them! It became more exciting when I showed the creations to our visitors, or when we went to stay with family on one of our very rare house escapes, and they wanted to buy them! Then it started to look like something new, some extra money I could make to allow us a few extra treats.

Any creative at all will know it takes a lot of materials when you first set up something you can make to turn any kind of profit. As I write this I am in the process of closing the door on my wedding stationery business for that very reason, it is hard to make money from raw materials easily (especially when weddings are restricted as they have been!).

For whatever reason, making pretty things has always been something I escape into, especially when I need to quiet my mind. I know that it's because it gives you a much more precise focus, and you can stop thinking the other million, billion things that fly around in your head the other 23 hours of the day – you are focused on learning the skill, threading the bead pattern onto the wire, or remembering the stitch combination, and the rest of your mind just goes quiet for a while.

When they say it's therapeutic, that's what they mean.

Calligraphy

I've been very interested in learning the skill of letter writing for years, but for some reason, I have never invested the time in doing it properly, I prefer to figure stuff out for myself I think that's why. But I am going to tell you now about a huge calligraphy project I once undertook which got me through a very dark, difficult time in my life.

When I was just 20 years old, I gave birth to my beautiful second-born son, Jay. Sadly, he didn't make it into this world and was stillborn one day after he was due. It is something I have talked about a lot over the quarter of a decade, and faced up to, learned to live with, and owned as part of my journey. But that has been incredibly tough.

The year it happened, 1996, was the bleakest, most emotionally challenging year of my whole life. We lost him in January, and so as you can imagine, the time that followed was coloured by his loss. Talking (as I have also covered in a different chapter) was one of the things that undoubtedly got me through a lot of that year, but again I turned to creative pursuits. In fact, in the days when I was preparing to give birth to him, with no knowledge of what was to come, I sat carefully handwriting what were supposed to be his birth announcement cards, one in pink with the girl's name we had chosen, and one in blue, with his name on them. We never got to send these, the blue one is kept, as a memory of the life I once dreamed of. Once the initial shock wore off, which obviously took some months, I turned again to calligraphy style handwriting as a hobby. It was all about him, in those dark weeks and months. I would write him letters and poems as and when I felt the need. In the run-up to the first anniversary of his death, and first birthday (just one day apart) I set about 'A book for Jay'. Every single letter I had written him, the poems and very personal letters written for him by our families, and all my poems, plus lyrics to meaningful songs too, all got handwritten and colours added and carefully crafted, with love.

When you lose someone so close to you, especially when it is so sudden, unexpected, and unexplained, that love feels like it has nowhere to go. As a 20-year-old young woman who felt like she had failed at the most basic, fundamental thing in the world, creating another life, I wanted his life and existence to mean something. I realise now, 25 years later that it means everything, of course, it does, but at the time I just couldn't get past that, I struggled so much with his loss. Even though I had my firstborn alive and well, I, myself was lost too, for a long time. Focusing some of my healing time on creating something helped me to feel as though I wasn't completely worthless. I know that those around me tried to help me see that, but I could never explain how I was feeling because it was all so senseless. When I wrote and worked on these projects, I felt as though it connected me to him in a deeper more meaningful way.

Maybe that's exactly what it did, at the time.

The truth is there is no right or wrong way to get through something, no one can ever tell you how you should or shouldn't be feeling, because we are all unique and have walked a different path. How you find your way through it will be right for you at that moment. If you want to write it out, then do it. I know that working on 'A Book for Jay' gave me some sense of fulfilment I was so clearly lacking at the time. There are lots of elements to doing 'proper' calligraphy, you can use embossing powders, feather quills, your stylised form of lettering, there are different 'set' styles, such as gothic, roman, etc but the best way to find out is to experiment. It's a fairly cheap hobby to get started with, especially if you look up tutorials on youtube!

Go for it.

Cross stitch

Not to be mistaken with embroidery, (completely different, not my forte at all), I do love cross stitch, because you just do what you're told. It's a bit like colour by numbers but with little 'xs' using the specified colours of embroidery thread. I could get lost in a cross-stitch pattern for hours, I truly feel like it's something almost anyone can do (you are welcome to disagree!).

Again it was something that started in my late teens, after I left home, with the gift of a little kit of a cute badger design – I had a real thing for badgers for years ever since bumping into one in the middle of the night on girl guide camp when I was about 13 years old. I just loved the look of this kit, it wasn't huge and overwhelming, probably about the size of a coaster, and it just had these cute little pops of colour on it which would break up the pattern. The only thing I would say was that I was ever so prone to the threads getting crossed over and tangling up, which could get annoying, but there are plenty of things you can get that stop this from happening.

It starts quite slow, especially if you try what I did when I first started and only use the colour that's on your needle, you can have little bits of pattern here there, and everywhere. It all depends on how exactly you want to finish the pattern, I don't recommend doing it this way because there's every chance you will miscount the little squares of fabric, and then it's very hard to undo it!

Nonetheless, I do enjoy cross stitch, there are all kinds of different patterns you can get, kits, make your own – it became another thing I, of course, had to do differently, there are those called 'birth samplers' which had the name, weight, date of your child's birthday, and of course after losing a child these things can make you quite mad, so I chose to make my design of that too – it included little angels, symbols that were significant to us at the time, whatever text we wanted - not 'welcome to the world' - which is what is quite often used and I felt like by doing it this way, I was making it much more unique. This was important to me. You could do them in any kind of style you wanted if it was your choice. With computer programs being so much more advanced these days I am sure it would be much easier to do as well.

You can always choose something that works with your situation. Personally, since becoming cat owners in 2016 I had not been as tempted by the idea of knitting or anything involving lots of long stringy type things! So I have had to reorganise my space – Otherwise, it would probably push me over the edge and take away from the therapy I was seeking, haha.

Something I discovered recently is that creativity is also linked to spirituality. I never really understood this until now but it completely makes sense to me. Unlocking your creativity makes more space in your world for good feelings to come forth and with that you find more intuitive thoughts come through, your unique inner wisdom can be heard louder and clearer. More on that in the second half of the book!

Back to the present day

It's fascinating to me that since I wrote the initial thoughts for this chapter, I have found my way back into enjoying my cross-stitch. I felt compelled to go and find one of my half-finished projects from many years ago and get stuck into doing it again. During the very strange time of Covid 19, a lot of people have turned to things they find therapeutic as the entire world has completely slowed right down (it's bliss if you can find the positive in it). I felt the urge to pick up some cross-stitch so I went for a rummage in the cupboard where no one dares to tread (in my sons converted attic room, so basically the only loft space available to us) and found a whole bag of half-finished projects I had put to one side for a rainy day. I did not imagine a pandemic would be that rainy day.

The first thing I did was complete a fully knitted but not yet sewn together tea cosy I started some 8 years or so ago, and I was thrilled to realise that there wasn't a lot left to do, a lovely sunny day in the garden and it was my time to get this sorted! I just love this tea cosy now I have finally finished it and it reminds me just how much joy these projects have brought to my world over the years.

Now for the half stitched cross stitch patterns...

I returned first to a pattern I had started in the 90s, a really long but very cute festive penguin one. I made it my mission to complete it in time for Christmas 2020 and because there is so much more 'free' time to go around just at the moment, I blooming well did it. Now I am very close to finishing a gorgeous 'Baby Blue Jays' cross-stitch pattern, the name says it all, and I am just days away from finishing it. *Amendment to this section:* It's at least 2 months since I wrote this, and that pattern is now finished and I'm halfway through another one. Just loving the creative process!

I have loved getting so involved in crafts again, it has truly always been one of my most loved activities, but I lost the intention for some years. Having a creative business in the wedding industry sort of took care of it, but I missed doing it 'just for me'.

The thing is, when you take care of your needs as a priority, you never know how your life will change.

PS: DON'T FORGET TO GRAB YOUR BONUS MATERIAL!

If you enjoyed the exercise at the end of the self-care section in chapter one, don't forget the bonus workbook I've created just for you!

Visit **bit.ly/YGTworkbook**

Where you can download your very own fully complimentary PDF workbook with simple exercises you can do to accompany each and every section of this book! They will help you get clear on what you *need* to do right now to better support yourself – and I'll be there cheering you on.

The power of Friendships

When you're used to being the strong one

The 'go-to' friend that people know they can count on, it can be tough to admit that you are the one who needs help and support. No matter what the situation you are in, you need – you deserve - to know that you have those people you can count on too, they won't be 'judgy', they will listen to you, they may give you some advice, but you know whatever happens you can trust them to be there.

I call these people my cheerleaders. They are rooting for me to succeed, with no ulterior motive.

I didn't always truly have that sense of belonging, I always felt like the 'extra' friend in the group, and if I'm honest, I think there is still an element of that sometimes now, but as we grow older, we find ourselves more knowing that being part of a group isn't necessarily the only way.

Here is a perfect example of this.

When I turned 12 years old, we had this amazing outing planned - my dad had the coolest job around! He worked in the Mars chocolate factory (we always had a stash of their bars and treats in the cupboard) and had organised for us to go there on a tour. You had to be 12 years old to go on these, something to do with health and safety I think, and my school friends were so looking forward to it. There were 7 of us, plus my sister took a couple of friends too and my parents (I think they came around with us, some of the details are a little hazy, to be honest). All in all, there were 12 of us for this tour, and when we got to the factory and they talked us through everything, they said we'd need smaller groups – so split into 2 groups of 6. Do you know what happened? My 6 friends from school made a cosy little group, and I felt like I got cast aside! I can say that now because let's be honest, when you're 14 like my sister was, it isn't cool to have your little sister tagging along all the time, and there I was, my friends had kept their perfectly round number and it felt as though they weren't truly bothered if I was there or not. It was MY birthday outing, we had been through junior school together and so for years we had looked forward to this adventure, but now it didn't seem to matter if I even got to be part of it with them. I was hurt, and it took away from my experience of going around the factory that I had looked forward to for so long. Just to clarify, I am still friends with some of these girls, so I'm definitely not holding it against them!

I'll be completely honest now, when I sat down to write this chapter, I hadn't even remembered this episode, so it isn't like its something that I clung onto all these years, but that is the power of writing from your heart!

So when more difficult stuff comes along in life, you need to know your closest friends will have your back! I've always worked better in individual friendships, to be honest, being an empath I am not always the greatest in larger groups but I liked to feel I belonged. As the years have passed, I have filtered out those who have stopped me from feeling protected.

If you are struggling, it is super important (I actually cannot stress this enough) to know that those you have chosen to support you have your best intentions at heart. There are several reasons for this and that, I suppose is the reason I felt this chapter was important – it can make or break you if you are constantly wondering whether or not those by your side aren't just waiting for you to turn round so they talk about you behind your back! These conflicting emotions will drain you when your energies are probably (almost definitely) best saved for dealing with the problem at hand.

When my marriage collapsed in 2015, I was blessed to be surrounded by beautiful shining lights.

My best friend Helen (from the age of 5, a true bestie who is never afraid to speak her mind but will still support me regardless, and boy do I wish we had some of our heart to hearts earlier than we did, but that's probably another book!) had offered to come and stay on more than one occasion -there then came a time when I knew I would need her, I needed to know that she could hold me up if I was unable to do it myself. And that was all I wanted, we talked, we drank, we pampered ourselves, we talked some more, but honestly, those 3 days she stayed with me were like a month in therapy!

I had several very close friends who could barely believe what was happening to me, but showed up, with meals, offers of childcare, or were just there to listen – on more than one occasion they even helped me complete wedding stationery orders for clients when I could barely see for my tears!

And then some had me questioning things – not just my decisions, that is hard enough when your world has been turned upside down! – but had me questioning what their role in my life was? I didn't need their 'approval' for what I was dealing with, for feeling how I felt, I most certainly didn't need to feel as though they were just waiting to watch me make an unholy mess of everything. I think the truth was at this moment in time I barely felt I could trust my judgement but I didn't need to be wasting those precious extra brain cells on trying to figure out why they suddenly wanted to step up? They asked a lot of questions, which I was too exhausted for, and I didn't truly feel that they 'got it'.

Sometimes you don't need to feel like people 'get' what you are doing, but if you don't feel you can trust them, it probably will not help you in the long run.

Everybody comes from a different place, with a different experience, and if your energy is shifted away from the moment by someone who is eventually only going to drain you, you need protection from that. I wish I could have seen these people for who they were at the time, it was like I found myself with a 'false' safety net. They just wanted the gossip, it felt to me, they weren't truly interested in the impact of what was happening. It wore me down. I spent months feeling as though I was seeking their approval – another one of those groups where I always felt like the outsider, the latecomer. None of that matters when you have true friends who don't really care when you showed up in their life, they are just glad that you did.

This I suppose is a word of warning to you. If you are struggling or suffering a loss or a big change in your life, be cautious not to open up to just anyone who will listen. Not everyone is going to know how to respond, they may end up filling your head with more questions than answers, and this can be difficult to navigate, counter-productive, and really bad for your mental health.

It's also fair to say that not everyone knows how to support you, so if someone goes quiet when you need them, try not to judge this. Simply let them know that it's okay if they don't know how to support you, but that you value their friendship for what it is. Maybe they don't agree with your decisions at that time but know that you don't need to hear it right now – sometimes that is enough, valuable friendships are hard to come by but they are not based on always saying or doing the 'right' thing.

I want you to surround yourself with the kind of circle you know you can count on, however small. You are worth it. The size of your crowd isn't what matters anyway, it's the quality of the friendship that counts. Do you know who you can rely on 100% and will be there for you no matter what? Fill your crowd with those people, rather than a half-arsed effort of people who just like knowing what it is you have going on just so they have something to talk about down the pub.

Take heart that if you are young (by that I mean thirty or less!) it can take time to figure this stuff out, friendships and our expectations of them can change significantly over the years.

When you are grounded in yourself, in your own identity of who you are and what you want from life, those who are consistently by your side through the good times and bad will show up at the right moments, with no agenda. They will call you unexpectedly when you feel too sad to pick up the phone, ask how you are AND listen for the answer – not just wait to find an opportunity to talk about themselves.

These are your cheerleaders, remember them.

PS: DON'T FORGET TO GRAB YOUR BONUS MATERIAL!

If you enjoyed the exercise at the end of the self-care section in chapter one, don't forget the bonus workbook I've created just for you!

Visit **bit.ly/YGTworkbook**

Where you can download your very own fully complimentary PDF workbook with simple exercises you can do to accompany each and every section of this book! They will help you get clear on what you *need* to do right now to better support yourself – and I'll be there cheering you on.

The Second Half!

Welcome, oh wonderful one.

Although I have lightly touched on some more spiritual-based principles in the first half of the book, I felt it made more sense to have a separate section here, so you would have some idea what to expect. Maybe!

You probably have an idea of spiritual types as being a bit 'out there', usually because that's how we are portrayed. For me, living a life led by spiritual principles simply means I am in touch with that which has been sent to help me make my life better, more balanced, calmer, clearer, and more purposeful. It isn't like it's something we choose, it usually finds its way to us, and that is why you won't find any 'preachy' tactics in this book. Everyone has their own understanding and beliefs and that is absolutely fine! I am not going to pretend to be the font of all knowledge on any topic, nobody is. What I do promise is that the sprinkling of spirituality you will find here can simply be something that you try for yourself to see how it makes you feel.

That's all. I want to help you feel good.

If it doesn't feel natural to you to adopt any of these methods, no problem!

I am a firm believer in 'what's for you won't go by you' - so if this is something good and meant for you to explore, you have information readily available to help you on your way.

Enjoy the journey.

You've got this!

Mindfulness

The art of mindfulness can be a little open to interpretation.

You can do anything mindfully if you choose to.

For now, here is a definition which I feel describes for me what is important about it (there are many experts available to give you a much more detailed explanation, such as Ruby Wax, who is very informed on the subject) but I rather liked this one:

'Mindfulness means maintaining a moment-by-moment awareness of our thoughts, feelings, bodily sensations, and surrounding environment, through a gentle, nurturing lens'.

Sounds pretty good to me?

It is a form of awareness, applying your conscious attention to whatever you are focusing on, in that moment. Not allowing your thoughts to be distracted by the 'background' noise that we have come to know in the 21st century, without placing any judgement on yourself when that does happen. It's definitely an art form which takes a lot of practice to 'bring yourself back' to whatever it is that you are mindfully doing, or focusing on.

For one, you have to remind yourself that you are doing this, without letting your thoughts drift off once you notice you're not 'being mindful'. You simply acknowledge that you have caught yourself drifting, and bring your attention back to the moment you're in. Without any judgement for the drifting part.

For another, it can be hard to achieve if you are in a place where you can be easily distracted, especially if you are just starting out.

As I have already mentioned, I am not purporting to be a mindfulness expert, by any stretch of the imagination. But I do know that learning just how much was available to me to help me calm my mind and soothe my soul, made a huge difference to my outlook over many years.

In a similar vein, discovered more as a tool for my business, I discovered some fascinating techniques that can be applied to help you feel more like you have a handle on things. One of them is to stop trying to multi-task! It can be extremely bad for you, using lots of precious energy on too many things at a time and not really doing any of them thoroughly or seeing them through to completion! I have put a link to a great book for learning more about this in the Useful links section, it's called 'Getting Things Done' and is labelled as the art of stress-free productivity.

So whilst not entirely related to spiritual practices I am sure you can see that slowing down your mind in whatever you are doing is super helpful to your wellbeing, and that's what I'm all about, at the end of the day!

With that in mind, I've got a tiny exercise you can try right now

to see if you can just begin to focus your mind on just one thing, which will immediately help you to slow down the internal chatter.

Ready?

In a space where you won't be disturbed, light a tealight or candle - somewhere away from obvious hazards such as curtains (hey, I don't mean to be patronising, I'm just being a responsible author).

Focus on the flickering flame - nothing else.

Watch it dance in front of you, wavering and steadying again. Just focus on the flame, nothing else.

You will become totally absorbed in the light of this candle (ooh I'm starting to feel like some TV hypnotist - definitely not my forte) and how it moves and dances all by itself. It will become the sole focus of your attention, and any other thoughts that previously took up your busy headspace start to fade.

Feeling calmer?

The action of mindfully focusing on just one object or action (you can do this when chopping vegetables, walking, even just sitting on a park bench and watching the trees in the breeze) calms the grey matter in your mind (technical term for this is the Amygdala, which is the area that deals with stress) and in time it starts to reduce, hence your stress levels decrease. Magical eh?

Practiced consistently, even in very small amounts, this tool can be incredibly useful at giving you a bit of a 'time-out' from the daily stresses and help you slow down, even if just enough to get some perspective - I am sure you can already see how useful that can be!

I can't wait to find out if you've tried out any of these wonderful tools I have shared throughout the book - my social media links will be available at the end so we can connect if you want to. I'd love to hear from you.

You've got this!

BONUS MATERIAL!!!

If you enjoyed the exercise at the end of this chapter, I've got some great news for you!

There's plenty more where that came from!

Visit **bit.ly/YGTworkbook**

Where you can download your very own fully complimentary PDF workbook with simple exercises you can do to accompany each and every section of this book! They will help you get clear on what you need to do right now to better support yourself – and I'll be there cheering you on.

Meditation

My journey of meditation

Started back in 2016 when my life was truly getting ready to shift a gear or 5. Understanding it to simply be a different way to relax and switch off from the battle of my daily life, I was soon to find out it could offer me so much more!

Before I tell you about my own personal journey and share some valuable tips with you, I wanted to let you know some brilliant news – meditation is really good for your health! It can help slow down your heart rate, relieve you of potentially damaging internal chatter, improve pain tolerance (I once knew a lady who meditated through a major operation, rather than undergo a general anaesthetic), and gift you with much more clarity and focus. What's not to love?

I have dipped in and out of meditation over the last few years because I start to feel better and think I don't need to do it any more…a common mistake! But honestly, the peace of mind, the insights I receive, and the mental clarity it brings to me - worth its weight in gold!

Now you might have a certain picture in your head of someone meditating. I just bet they have buddha like qualities, burn tons of incense sticks, sit on some kind of stripey cotton rug, and chant, don't they? Wrong.

Don't misunderstand me, there are very good reasons to do all of these things, should you choose to, and this is usually guided by finding your way to what it is you need at that moment. But honestly, in 4 years, I can count on one hand the number of times I have sat with my back straight, palms facing upward – which, by the way, is something that can help, we can come to that later...

There are different ways you can choose to meditate, I think it depends on how disciplined you are.

Personally – I am being honest here – I am often not that good at concentrating on one thing at a time! That's just me. For me, guided meditations work better, because at least there is someone there giving you some idea of how to begin, what you can be thinking about/visualising to help you on your way, and talking you through it.

But there is also self-led meditation, an art form of relaxing your body, quietening your mind, and asking for yourself what it is you want to get from the meditation. You can have music set to one side perfect for this, or you might prefer the silence. My situation is that we live on a rather busy main road (I did love the total peace we had when the country was in our first lockdown, does that make me weird?) and I find it hard to achieve complete silence here which is probably why I often prefer the guided ones as you can block out more noise!

The best news is, it doesn't have to be something you do for hours and hours. You can, but if 10 minutes or less, once a day is all you have, that is more than enough. Just that little window of time can be enough to get your mind cleared, help you feel calmer and ready to go about your day.

I tend to do mine at the beginning of the day, it starts me off with a positive mindset and I always feel like whatever I do that day, I am supported and have focused my energies on the right things. If I am having a particularly difficult day, there is no reason why I can't just do a quick brief meditation during the day too, and before I lay down to sleep if necessary. It does you no harm at all. I don't usually feel the need for all 3 but have been known to do a second round later on when I am struggling, or need to shift my focus to something new.

The magical thing I have found when I find this inner peace, and am aligned with my goals and dreams is that I receive what are known as 'downloads'. It's the hardest thing to describe but put simply it's as if whatever you need to know that day just arrives in your mind in a flash and you know and trust that it makes complete sense. I go through phases of receiving these, and in the last few weeks, since starting to focus more on my heart led goals and dreams, that of helping more people find their way forward and eventually find their bliss, generating more written work, and more spiritually led work, I am receiving them more and more. The majority of my first book, Onward and Upward simply flowed from my fingertips and writing it was effortless because I knew what message it was I needed to share. To know that my words helped so many people – how can all those 5* reviews be wrong? – such a powerful feeling.

If you are thinking of giving it a try, here are a few tips for how to put yourself in the frame of mind that allows inspiration, love, and support to flow.

Medical note/disclaimer: Don't ever attempt to listen to a meditation recording if you are driving or operating heavy machinery, unlikely I know but it does still need to be said.

Time of day:

It's entirely up to you when you choose to begin your meditation journey. As I have said before, I find it sets me up for the day, but if that point in time is not the calmest for you, perhaps you have children to feed, get ready for the school run, work commute, dog to walk, etc then it will be difficult to imagine slotting that into your morning. Maybe just before bed feels more achievable to you? Why not give it a go. Of course, it doesn't have to be the same time every day, either! Just try and make the promise to yourself that you will attempt a short meditation once a day.

Frequency:

If you can work meditation into your daily routine, I promise you, you will feel the benefits very quickly. This is why it can be a good idea to have a regular time of day that you do it. I have a little 'self-care' checklist for the mornings which includes meditation. It isn't always the first thing I do before leaping out of bed but if I can squeeze it in there, then I do. However, if you are thinking 'no way, every day?' that's fine. Once a week would be better than nothing if it's something you are working towards in your life goals. But try and have a bit of an idea of how often you would like to aim for.

Length:

Look, I will be honest with you here – no one who needs a book like this has the time to meditate for an hour every day (do you?) and you really don't need to. There are guided meditations you can do, that take you on a bit of a journey, they often take longer to work your way through but if you are thinking to yourself 'this is going on forever' you will not be entirely in the moment of the meditation and more distracted, which does no one any good. My daily meditation practice is usually no more than a 10 minute one, I have many different types of recordings to choose from, and more often than not I will go on to do another, and then perhaps another. It is down to personal choice as well as the amount of time available to you. Try not to shoe-horn it in if you can though, because it might not be as beneficial to you.

Type:

Guided, written, spoken, helping with your sleep, an abundance meditation – the list goes on.

There are many different forms of meditation available.

As I have already said, the guided ones can be really good if you are just starting (I have been doing it for 4 years or more and still go for guided ones more often than not), what I will say is that you have to find one that resonates, and a voice that you find you can connect to. Nothing worse than an accent you can't stand or any aspect that will distract you from hearing what they have to say. You can always write one yourself and voice record it into your phone to playback! Your own voice is meant to be the most powerful thing to hear. I plan to record my own very soon, check out my social media pages if you want to keep updated!

You can read the **written meditations** available and repeat those to yourself as you drift, not as helpful from personal experience because you have to memorise them – but maybe reinforcing the positive messages often associated with guided meditations is your thing, in which case, brilliant!

Sleep stories and meditations:

Can be fantastically powerful, as the words you hear while you drift off and find yourself in the land of nod will really get into your subconscious and start to take root, which is perfect if those messages are what you need to hear. Something I have found with this which doesn't work for me is that I like to switch off my devices at night. So if you are listening to something to help you sleep, it can be harder to achieve that. Check out the detail below about 'Do Not Disturb' settings on your device.

Abundance meditations:

These are good if you are working on your financial freedom and any goals surrounding that. Just like any beliefs, the more positive messages you can affirm to yourself, in many different ways, can start to help change your mindset around money. Good work to do alongside this is understanding your money story (here we go again, I definitely have more books in me after this one...) but that is something for another day, let's get back to the meditations.

Music:

This is particularly significant if you are attempting to meditate by yourself, without guidance. Find a soothing recording that transports you away from the busy-ness of your world. Gentle chiming, water trickling, waves lapping gently, birds tweeting. These lovely, soothing sounds will help guide you to a place of peace and sound mind, and you will probably start to associate them with your meditation practice when you hear them in the outside world too, giving you a further boost of relaxation and calm. I find it better to have just instrumental sounds rather than songs, but truthfully it's whatever works for you. None of this is a prescribed measure, as I have already said.

Smells:

Maybe you have familiar smells that trigger a memory of something relaxing that can help you with your routine. If you like a scented candle (who doesn't?) light one of those, if you are really into the incense sticks there are some great scents to choose from and if you want to go a bit further on your spiritual journey there is always white sage, which is used for 'smudging', cleansing the space of negative energy and clearing a path for good to enter. I do love white sage myself – you need to open a window if burning this though as it allows the negativity you are clearing to leave the room.

Routine:

Having a short list of things you do before you settle down to meditate can really help with your practice. Whether it is just choosing a quiet spot, making yourself a herbal tea, lighting that scented candle. Start to do these things as part of your practice and it will soon feel like a treat you are giving yourself rather than 'just another thing to do'. Recently I set aside a drawer with all my meditation-related stuff in it, so I can access it all easily and get in the zone. Maybe you have a notebook at the side to note down any flashes of inspiration that come to you in the moment, so you can jot them down as soon as you are finished.

Space:

Do you have some idea of a quiet spot where you can sit to do your meditation? Having space where you can ground yourself by keeping your feet firmly planted on the floor is an excellent idea. But there is no right or wrong. You're probably now thinking 'heeeelp, I don't have anywhere to go', don't worry about it! Honestly. About 95% of my meditations are done lying on the bed. The reason for this? Our home is a very noisy place, with a teenager and young adult on the autistic spectrum, quiet time is getting extremely hard to come by. Even when they are not in the room, you can always hear them, making their odd noises, getting frustrated with the cat (for being a cat…), disagreeing, shouting at their gaming friends online… it's just a hive of activity. However, we have somehow managed to enforce this unspoken rule, that if the master bedroom door is shut, they knock first, and wait for an answer. And I will be honest now, sometimes I just don't answer! And that's okay, I know the house isn't burning down and the distractions usually come at such random moments that I would never have the time to do any of these things if I kept looking at these as barriers. To some that might sound harsh, but my meditation practice has now become such a non-negotiable that I know I HAVE to make it a priority for that brief window of time. We all feel the benefits, too, so it isn't at all selfish.

Prioritising a space to do something for just a tiny window of time gives you a huge confidence boost that for once, you are putting yourself at the top of the pile – and if you have already read my chapter on self-care, you will know just how important that is!

Switch off distractions:

In this technological day and age, this is a tough one!

Most of my guided meditations are stored on a 'cloud'. Which means I access them off my phone. Which as I have already mentioned, means I have to have my phone on. Whether I am wearing headphones or not, this can be a terrible distraction. It was so worthwhile, spending just a few minutes setting everything up to get the best use out of the 'do not disturb' function. This meant selecting some of my 'preferred contacts', initial calls don't get put through but if they ring back (which usually means it is more urgent, right?) it will come through.

No pings from social media come through while I am meditating, no email alerts, all I can hear is the recording. Once I had got my head around how to do this, I knew that I could drift quite happily without worrying I was being irresponsible (and that too is why I have detailed here exactly how I did it, it won't take you long to master if you need to, promise).

It's also important to let anyone else in the house know that for that few minutes you wish not to be disturbed. Allowing ourselves distractions is a sign of the times, unfortunately, but I am working super hard right now on just focusing on the one thing I am doing and no other. It isn't always achievable but it can be done, just believe you can do it – know you are worth it - and you will find a way!

Be in the moment:

Above everything else, try really hard to just focus on this gift you are giving yourself, that of a bit of quality 'you' time. Meditating is all about quietening your busy mind so if you catch your thoughts drifting, acknowledge it, and bring yourself back to the task in hand, that of allowing yourself to just 'be'. Whatever you do, don't judge yourself (even if unintentionally) for getting distracted. Just bring yourself back to the task at hand, and start from there.

Don't be scared:

A lot of people - often those who haven't tried it - think meditation is a bit of a hippy practice, which is the reason why I have included it in this section of the book - but I know from personal experience that it really isn't something to be feared. I am happiest when I have managed a little window of quiet time doing just this one thing, it puts everything in its place for the rest of the day and helps me to cope. It doesn't mean you are going off on some spiritual journey that you don't understand – not if you don't choose to anyway – but what it will do is gift you with the knowledge that you can take control of a stressful situation by taking yourself away from it, just for a brief time, and get some perspective. You can go as deep as you like with it.

If you are more in touch with your spiritual side, it is helpful to know that it's a really good way to get in touch with your intuition. Your inner voice will more than likely become louder the quieter your mind becomes. As I mentioned earlier, the palms facing upward is quite a specific thing to do, it allows the positive energy to enter in and help you find your way forward to clearer, calmer thoughts and more guidance will come through, whether you expected it to or not.

You might even begin to enjoy it! I love my meditation time, and am honing the craft more every day – it's like the best gift you can give yourself.

And you so deserve it!

PS: DON'T FORGET TO GRAB YOUR BONUS MATERIAL!

If you enjoyed the exercise at the end of the mindfulness chapter, don't forget the bonus workbook I've created just for you!

Visit **bit.ly/YGTworkbook**

Where you can download your very own fully complimentary PDF workbook with simple exercises you can do to accompany each and every section of this book! They will help you get clear on what you *need* to do right now to better support yourself – and I'll be there cheering you on.

Affirmations

Stories we tell ourselves

Whether we are aware of these or not, even in our subconscious, can have a huge impact on our wellbeing. If we can make a conscious effort to make these stories positive ones, the change in our outlook is undeniable.

When I first began working with a life coach in 2016, I could not really grasp what she was trying to tell me, which was that by reinforcing stories that made my life feel better, my world would start to shift. I had paid her money to help me, so I did what she told me.

I thought long and hard about how I wanted to feel in my life (which was an extreme contrast to how I actually was feeling at that time, things were pretty bleak, my marriage was failing, 2 of my kids hated each other, they were suffering with their mental health and couldn't be left alone, I was in debt up to my eyeballs) so trying to imagine feeling anything other than just this crap from day to day, was quite tough.

Nevertheless, I adopted one of her strategies, which was to turn these around into positives, which was the opposite of what I was actually experiencing – I wanted to feel joy again, I wanted to feel free, I wanted peace. Doesn't sound like much to ask, does it? The agreement was to put entries in my diary every single day that told me how happy, free, and calm I felt. To believe that everything was okay (even though the evidence was extremely to the contrary) and keep telling myself this story, morning, noon, and night. To set reminders on my phone so that if I caught myself thinking or feeling bad, I focused on this outcome.

It was TOUGH. When you are presented with situations on a daily basis that tell you (not necessarily in words) that you are failing, it's very hard not to feel like a failure. It's hard not to listen to that narrative and keep focusing on the polar opposite. Especially if you spend your time with someone who seems to think you have lost the plot and who did you think you were, deserving of being happy anyway?

But you know what? I did it despite all that. I wanted to see what was possible. I needed something to change so badly.

These little post-its with lovely uplifting messages about how I dreamed I would actually feel one day were dotted around my home, inside my bathroom cabinet, on the fridge, in my home office – where I would see them often, and be reminded of what I was working towards.

I would write about how I was going to feel but I had to work hard to adapt it to that 'make-believe' where you imagine you are already experiencing it. That was hard, but I believed in what I had been told, I had no choice really. The alternative was to drudge through the hell I found myself living in and continue to struggle on a daily basis, with my sons, with my estranged husband, with my whole life, actually.

My favourite thing to do now with affirmations is to make pretty screen savers for my phone (yes, really, it has to look pretty, even more inspiring that way) or use the gorgeous card decks you can buy. I use these daily, ground myself, take some time and ask what I need to hear today, and then draw a beautiful card with the kind of uplifting message that just keeps you believing good things are coming – always.

If you take one thing away from this book, it could simply be that you choose to remind yourself daily that you are worthy of love, of feeling loved, of feeling good, that you can find these words, read them to yourself, and know that you deserve good things. Always.

Just recently we discovered a lovely song that talks about how you get what you give, and you *can* be completely loved even when you're by yourself. It was simply called 'Affirmation', by Savage Garden.

Here are a few examples of affirmations:

I live a happy carefree life every day

I am calm and relaxed

I feel happier and calmer than yesterday

My life is changing for the better

I live a life that makes my heart sing

I love my life and everyone who matters in my life loves me

I make positive changes to my world daily.

Now I know that some of this feels really far away at the moment, but if you continue repeating these, or your own chosen ones consistently, several times a day if you can, you will really start to shift your mindset. Instead of telling yourself negative stories about everything that isn't working in your life, you replace them with positive ones and more positive energy will find its way to you, helping you really start to live out those feelings in your world.

Try it today – just go for it.

PS: DON'T FORGET TO GRAB YOUR BONUS MATERIAL!

If you enjoyed the exercise at the end of the self-care section in chapter one, don't forget the bonus workbook I've created just for you!

Visit **bit.ly/YGTworkbook**

Where you can download your very own fully complimentary PDF workbook with simple exercises you can do to accompany each and every section of this book! They will help you get clear on what you *need* to do right now to better support yourself – and I'll be there cheering you on.

The Law of Attraction

I'm really excited

To share with you what I have learned about the Law of Attraction in recent years.

It's a powerful tool that can change your outlook and increase the wealth of opportunities available to you, forever more, if you let it. If you've ever heard the phrases 'like attracts like', 'what you put out, you get back', and similar such phrases (karma is very likely to be on this list), then you are aware of the principle of the Law of Attraction, whether you realise it or not.

There are a few things that can help you better understand what it is, and how it works, but before I go into explaining those, as always, I've got a real-life experience (well, a few actually) to share. This one happened to me most recently and it still has me so excited about what's to come that I simply have to share it with you.

I'll set the scene.

It's Autumn 2020, we have experienced months of varying stages of isolation, being stuck indoors, people have struggled, businesses have collapsed, relationships and family life tested to the max. A year of transformation for many, undoubtedly. In my own world, it has been a time of huge change.

At the start of lockdown, back in March/early April, I made the difficult but necessary decision that it was time to stop promoting my wedding stationery business. I have worked hard on this business for many years, and although it was fantastic for working with my more creative side, the wedding industry can be one of the toughest industries to work in. As fate would have it, this was the best decision I could possibly have made.

2020 was the year everyone wanted to get married, myself and my fiancé Bruce included. A lot of couples had this picture-perfect idea of their anniversary date having nice symmetrical numbers in them, it just sounds so neat! Our reasons were different to that, but that was the plan. As it has turned out, there have been fewer weddings this year than there have been for many years. Social distancing and Covid-19 has seen to that. Weddings have been cancelled by law, it just couldn't be done as the country moved into lockdown. Then tiny gatherings of no more than 6 people were allowed, barely enough to allow for the legal minimum requirements. As you can imagine, it has been a very tough year for the industry as a whole, couples demanding deposits back for weddings that looked nothing like they had dreamed of. We experienced the same, and in late August made our own decision to postpone for another year too.

I digressed a little, that's what I do, I'm a storyteller

Anyhow, during those months, I began doing more of what you would call 'inner work'. Focusing on all the benefits available to me from this time of less work and more time to reflect and grow as a person. For weeks now I've been saying I don't quite know what I want to do in the future, but I want it to be good. I do know if I have to, I will go out and get an admin job, shop work, whatever it takes if we need to financially. I do a little admin work for Bruce's brand new handyman business (another beautiful development during lockdown, incredibly) and I have been working on this book while I dig deeper with all this soul work.

The best stuff often comes when you're not looking, I have much experience of that to share with you.

So instead of focusing on 'I want to find a job that brings me x, y or z' I have been working on the belief that the right things will come at the right time – I have been no more specific than that. I have focused on feeling good, raising my vibration (you what, now? I will come to that in a minute if it's new to you), working on my alignment, and continually putting one foot in front of the other. I have stuck to doing things that make me feel good, and every day, although some days have felt a little bleaker than others, I have found something good, somewhere.

It's focusing on those, showing gratitude for even the tiniest things, that can really help, you see.

What happened just 2 days before I sat down to write this chapter I never expected, it was magical. I had been waiting for the right words to come before I sat down and wrote it, I often do that, my books are never written from the beginning churning out page after page until I reach the end, it just isn't the way I do things.

I have mentioned earlier in the book that I am an active member of West Bridgford Tuneless Choir, a fab, fun choir focused completely on singing for enjoyment, not worrying about whether we can produce a note between us. I have often watched in awe as the smoothly run sessions (well, okay, sometimes there are tiny errors, it is run by humans, after all) take shape, thinking to myself I'd love to do that. In recent weeks positions have been made available, none of which suited me, but the thought fleetingly passed through my mind, I never said anything about it to anyone, and onward I went, focusing on feeling good, always.

IMAGINE MY SURPRISE when, out of absolutely nowhere, Nadine, the manager of the original (and the worst, their words, not mine) West Bridgford Tuneless choir sent me a message saying 'I've got some news - and an opportunity'. Well, our history with the choir is we have been very involved, myself from the first day they launched in January 2016, and Bruce when he joined, in particular being as bold as to approach the organisers to coordinate his proposal of marriage to me, in front of our many members (maybe as many as 100?) so we are fondly nicknamed the Tuneless Lovebirds among our singing friends, it's a very familiar place to us indeed, we are like one big happy tuneless family. Back to the story - I had a few ideas of what the opportunity might be, but never for a minute did I expect what happened next.

'We're moving away, and I'm looking for someone to replace me as Tuneless Choir Manager in West Bridgford'. Huh? That's not really what she's asking me, surely?

'I have been pondering a couple of people who might be suitable, but then it came to me, you are perfect for this, and I'm very much hoping you will consider it.'

I beg your pardon now? You would like me to be more involved with something I love as much as Tuneless Choir, and I'll get paid for it too? Seriously? I start to think she's got me muddled up with someone else.

THIS IS MY DREAM JOB!

I can't actually believe what I'm hearing, but right there in that moment, I am so excited I can hardly compose myself (I was crossing a busy main road at the time of the conversation, luckily I stayed focused and got to the other side safely), firstly because it is the MOST AMAZING opportunity, secondly because it's all the confirmation I needed, as if I needed any, that the Universe has been listening, and listening hard. I would never have dreamed of attempting to manifest something like this because I didn't think it would be possible.

Another addition to this story is that for the whole of 2020, I had to be ultra-careful with my finances, because of a court order which provided a means to a very messy end after my divorce. It was due to finish in January. When did they want me to officially start work?

Yep, you guessed it, January.

Wow. Just WOW.

I spend the rest of the day high as a kite, I want to shout from the rooftops I JUST MANIFESTED MY DREAM JOB - AND I DIDN'T EVEN APPLY FOR IT. In all the years I've been learning about and getting to grips with the Law Of Attraction, I have heard so many stories just like this.

In fact, exactly how I came about being in the most amazing relationship I have ever known with my soulmate Bruce was very similar indeed... it was exactly the right thing at the perfect moment, I just didn't realise it but because I was paying attention to my intuition I took the leap, and I have never regretted it for a moment. We connected with such a powerful energy that I just couldn't ignore it! There's so much more in my first book Onward and Upward about that, so I guess if you want to know more about manifesting your soulmate, or you love a good old-fashioned happy ever after you will just have to go and check it out for yourself.

So just as an example of how the Law of Attraction works when you are in complete alignment with your true purpose, living the life you were meant to live, there you have it.

Ask and it is given.

Feel like you should be careful what you ask for? Don't panic. There are some simple steps to manifesting only what is for the greater good, and I will share those with you now.

My first tips are as follows:

1.Work on your alignment.

What is alignment?

Put quite simply, it is the magic that happens when you are 'in tune', and listening to the whispers of your soul or your inner voice. When you are in alignment, you have those 'hoppy skippy' kinds of days where you feel anything is possible. I get them quite a lot. When you are living the life you are truly meant to live, and everything is in place to support that, everything flows. Opportunities, conversations, people, and experiences who are in alignment with you, find their way to you. What's for you, won't go by you.

That may all sound a little 'far-fetched', or out of reach for you right now – honestly, that was me, in 2016.

How do you get in alignment?

By choosing those things that make you feel good, that support your best state of being, your happy place, and continuing to choose them. While this doesn't always feel possible, considering your choices just a little more carefully most certainly is. If you are not sure whether something is right for you, that is often a sign – that 'gut instinct' is a lot more than just a saying. If something feels good for you, you feel it in your gut, that butterfly feeling like when you first fall in love. Your work choices, lifestyle choices, food, and drink choices, even choosing one activity over another can affect your alignment. Negative self-talk can dramatically impact your alignment. Low moods can bring about more low moods and bring your alignment with your true purpose right the way down. You can work on things to bring it back up again, which I will come to in a moment.

How do you stay in alignment?

Awareness is KEY. No one can ever be 100 % aligned, 100% of the time. Even the world-renowned spiritual coaches have down days, tough times, but knowing there are things you can do RIGHT NOW to bring yourself back up a level, can be enough to make a difference. Even when you are having a good day, there is nothing to stop you from continuing to do this inner work, to maintain your mood, to stay on track, and keep putting your best foot forward (actually that was almost the title of this book!) This is where the shifts take place, when you understand that it's time to keep going with the work. Often we stop doing something because we don't feel like it's working, but ironically that's exactly what we need to keep doing – that's where breakthrough happens.

2.Notice your vibration

I'm sorry, what now?

Vibration is all about how your body responds to things you are either in or out of alignment with. Everything in the universe vibrates at a frequency.

We talk about positive and negative and that's how it comes back around – something vibrating at a positive (higher vibration) attracts positive feelings, people, and situations. Just as something vibrating at a low or negative frequency attracts more negative. So the more work you do on raising the frequency your body vibrates at, the better you will feel.

And guess what raises your vibration?

Good-feeling thoughts and actions. Happy experiences and anything that makes you feel good.

When you become more aware of this, you start to notice how situations or people either align with your vibration, so they are a vibrational match, or they are on a totally different wavelength (see, I told you it was something you'd heard about, you just didn't realise it).

3.Fine-tune your choices accordingly

You may now be realising that some people, places, or situations really don't fit with how you pictured your life in the affirmations section – and that's okay. Take your time with this, but by noticing, observing, and acting accordingly, you will gradually find yourself lifting some of the fog and making different choices. You might even find something naturally fall away – and that's okay too.

I have left it until this point in the book to go into more detail because I realise there is a LOT of information here. Learning about and understanding how all of this fits together is going to be more than a one-time read thing so I have designed this book exactly so that you can find what relates to your situation at this moment in time. This is important because there's no way you can do all of the things I have listed – in fact, I advise against it.

Much of the time it is a journey through one methodology to another one and that is often the best way, finding what works for you right now, and going with it. Just play around with what feels good to you, the rest will fall into place, I promise.

You've got this!

PS: DON'T FORGET TO GRAB YOUR BONUS MATERIAL!

If you enjoyed the exercise at the end of the self-care section in chapter one, don't forget the bonus workbook I've created just for you!

Visit **bit.ly/YGTworkbook**

Where you can download your very own fully complimentary PDF workbook with simple exercises you can do to accompany each and every section of this book! They will help you get clear on what you *need* to do right now to better support yourself – and I'll be there cheering you on.

E.F.T (Emotional Freedom Technique/Tapping)

Just a few days after I began writing this book

I had one of those wobbles. Who on earth am I to try and give people self-care advice? Surely this information is already out there for anyone who wants it, why don't they just use google? And then I had a really rubbish Monday. It's currently lunchtime and I've been feeling totally out of whack just lately – so how on earth can I advise you to help yourself?

Because I am doing just that, all the time, right now. The news and everything has been dominated by Covid-19, this epic virus which has totally taken over all the social media feeds, our thoughts and feelings, it feels like it's all monopolised by talk of the virus. The world feels like a very bizarre place to be right now. It's uncertain, it can be unsettling, and pretty damn scary.

When all else fails, I force myself to get up and get on with it. But on this particular Monday, I just couldn't shift those negative thoughts – nothing specific, just struggling to lift myself up – feeling much if that makes sense. I know I am not alone in this either. I have read some quite horrifying statistics about the impact on mental health just recently, including one speaker I follow who said he'd been booked to give a talk to 40 secondary school students, all of whom had attempted suicide during the past fortnight amid our third

National Lockdown. 40 teenagers united by this stark reality who couldn't cope. Sometimes there just aren't words.

Now, I am a huge fan of Gabrielle Bernstein, I don't watch her live feeds all day, although I am in her monthly membership which has just been so amazing for resources and support - what she says makes a lot of sense to me, and I like her style. Especially because what she encourages is a faith of your own understanding - it's all inclusive no matter what you believe. Sometime during the earliest days of lockdown 1, she delivered a live anxiety calming workshop (online, where we all seem to hang out at this time) which was completely free - a lot of people are giving more than ever for free at the moment, it's keeping the world moving - and so I decided to tune into the recording of it.

Wow.

I had heard of E.F.T. (Emotional Freedom Technique) and experimented with it just a little around 2016 when my journey began, but I never went any further with it. Part of Gabby's transmission was working through some E.F.T. with you, simply tapping on the meridian points and self-calming with repeated phrases you work your way around the points demonstrated, tapping gently on each in turn, and talking through your feelings, acknowledging them, accepting them, making your peace with them, allowing them and honouring them as you work your way through.

Just 10 minutes of that and I felt so much better, it was instant, I can't even explain it but there it is. So I just thought I would share.

Almost 2 months after writing that opening paragraph, I feel like I am getting to grips with E.F.T. enough to share a simple introduction with you - I have also started studying it to get myself better acquainted.

The basic principles behind it are that by rating the 'issue' most bothering you right now, or blocking you from moving forward (we've all been there), tapping in your opening phrase which ideally starts with this:

"Even though I feel anxious (or sad, lonely, muddled, angry, whatever it is, you can choose your own wording) start first on the 'Karate chop' point with 3 fingers from the opposite hand, tapping gently several times.

Making your way around the meridian points using just your forefinger and middle finger now – the inner point of your eyebrow, the 'almond' outer corner of your eye, under your eye, under your nose (your upper lip), your chin, your collarbone, under your arm, and finally the very top of your head, you slowly but surely find that the positive reinforcement of accepting and then working through the feeling you are trying to deal with, combined with the tapping frees up the blocked energy at those points, allowing it to move more freely through your body, just as nature intended, and resetting a lot of the negative emotions and beliefs that you are holding in your body.

There are plenty of tutorial videos for this online but don't forget you can download the 'Heartfelt Approach' workbook (link at the end of the chapter) to find exercises that go into more detail! If you feel the need to get more of a visual guide I have also included a graphic here to show you the main tapping points.

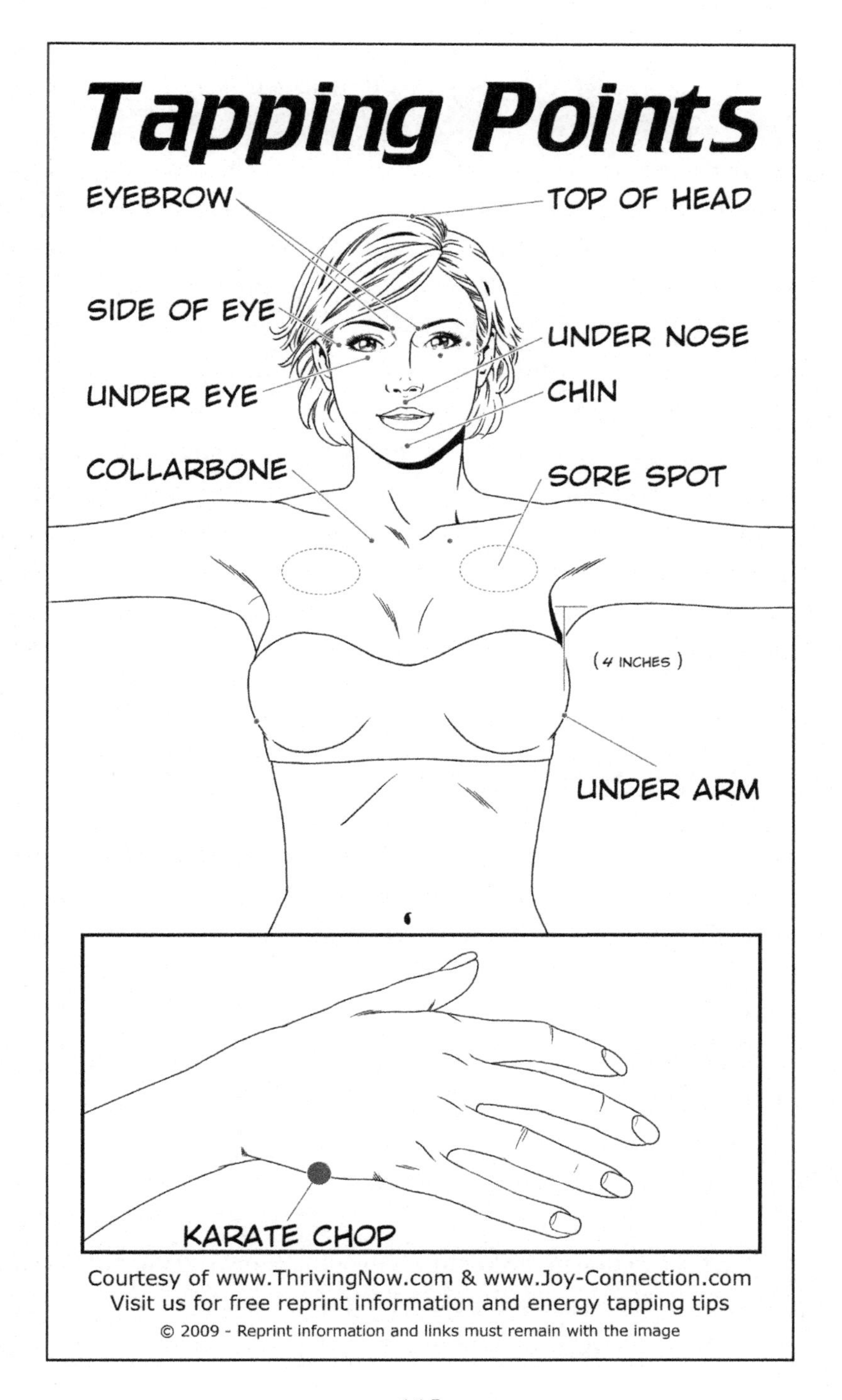
Tapping Points
EYEBROW
TOP OF HEAD
SIDE OF EYE
UNDER NOSE
UNDER EYE
CHIN
COLLARBONE
SORE SPOT
(4 INCHES)
UNDER ARM
KARATE CHOP
Courtesy of www.ThrivingNow.com & www.Joy-Connection.com
Visit us for free reprint information and energy tapping tips
© 2009 - Reprint information and links must remain with the image

Image courtesy of www.thrivingnow.com

There is no harm in ever trying out any of these techniques while you work out if they are the ones for you, or not. As you can tell from the wide range of techniques in this book, I have tried many different things over the years (and probably forgotten some of them on the way too!).

In writing about these seemingly unfamiliar techniques (that let's face it not everyone has heard of!) I am in my own way letting it be known to the world that I am on my spiritual journey and that in itself is a huge deal for me. We are all on our own journey and sometimes just facing up to these things can be very liberating. I will most certainly be 'tapping' on issues as they come up, as it can be a challenge to rise up against those who don't understand. That's okay too, it isn't their journey to understand. Being an empath has made it hard for me to know that it truly is okay not to worry about the opinions of others at such times. I take on a lot of other people's energy, worries, belief systems, and anxieties when it isn't my place to do so. These things can be replayed in your mind over and over again, with no way of shifting them out.

I started this morning by writing out how I was feeling about a certain situation, and the next step for me in that is to work on a phrase I can tap with so that I don't just go over and over a conversation until it wears me into the ground – I bet you know what I am saying?

I will consider just how much of an issue this is, is it a really strong feeling, so a 10/10? Or perhaps an 8 or a 9? Then I will begin.

I will use my opening 'set-up' phrase which may be something like 'Even though I feel frustrated, irritated, and confused, I deeply and completely love and accept myself'. I tap on the karate chop point of my right hand, repeating this phrase a further 2 times. Lightly tapping in the corner of my eyebrow above my nose with a finger, firmly but gently, I will repeat 'I am so frustrated'.

Lightly tapping again the outer corner of my eye, again firmly but gently, 'all this frustration'. Moving to above my upper lip 'I feel so irritated'.

Do you know just writing about this is helping me, even now!

Repeating those parts of the opening statement, accepting and owning up to how I am feeling, while slowly working my way around the meridian points will calm the Amygdala (that grey matter part of your brain linked with your emotions), keeping me present in the moment of all the irritation and frustration I am dealing with until I reach the crown point at the top of my head.

Time to reassess. Am I still at an 8 or a 9? Has it reduced?

Begin another round starting first with the eyebrow.

'I'm so pissed off about feeling like this' (because it does bug me that I get so irritated sometimes by the seemingly smallest things). Just underneath my eye 'All this irritation'. And so on. At the end of round 2, assess again. Maybe I have reduced it to a 5 or a 6?

Repeat until I feel the issue has come right down, ideally down to a 2 or below.

That may sound like quite a dramatic drop but just think of the benefits that will have on your mental health. You feel calmer, your breathing rate has reduced, your mind isn't quite so 'choppy', your energy not quite so fractured. The knock-on effect of this can be huge.

You can use this technique to help you work your way through a headache, or physical pain. Notice where in your body the pain is and set to work on that.

As I have sat writing this, quietly but confidently I know that eventually becoming certified in such a powerful technique is going to be pivotal in how I deliver my spiritual practice. I want to have a specific skill that I can share, to help others learn to cope better in difficult situations and I'm so excited that I found EFT again when I did. Already a very good friend of mine who has always been leagues ahead of me in her journey is excited to know how I can share what I am learning to help her move forward.

It sounds so simple. That's because it is.

So are you going to give it a try? What have you got to lose?

PS: DON'T FORGET TO GRAB YOUR BONUS MATERIAL!

If you enjoyed the exercise at the end of the self-care section in chapter one, don't forget the bonus workbook I've created just for you!

Visit **bit.ly/YGTworkbook**

Where you can download your very own fully complimentary PDF workbook with simple exercises you can do to accompany each and every section of this book! They will help you get clear on what you *need* to do right now to better support yourself – and I'll be there cheering you on.

Reiki

My Reiki healing journey

began before I truly understood what it was all about. It has undoubtedly contributed to my spiritual evolvement and helped me find the happy place I am in today.

I was drawn to a group programme in early 2017 with the powerful writing coach, author, and mentor Cassandra Farren (we have since worked on several different projects together, she is also on our guestlist for our forthcoming wedding) which was all about stepping into your power as a woman. Having recently begun a completely new chapter in my life as a single mum, and loving it, it spoke to me. I wanted to move forward from what had been a very complicated and drawn-out separation healthily, to begin to heal properly and not allow myself to be held back by my past. It was important to me because I knew that possibly one day in the future I would be ready to find a new love - definitely not at that time - however, to do that successfully I had to work on myself, had to had to had to, no question. Cassandra had previously gifted me a copy of her first book 'The Girl who Refused to Quit' when we first connected and I felt she really understood about the journey I was on right now.

I didn't really understand what Reiki healing - also known as 'Energy healing' - actually was at the time. Reiki is a Japanese technique that helps reduce stress and relax you. Traditional 'hands on' healing doesn't even involve any actual physical hands on you, the energy flows from source, through your healer via the palms of their hands to the areas where you need the healing most. From a certified healer who is guided to send you the most beautiful, peaceful energy during a session. Working their way from your head to your feet, passing over each individual chakra point (the individual energy centres throughout your body), the energy sent to you is there to soothe and clear any energy blocks. We all experience these blocks throughout our lives, often on a daily basis, triggered by experiences and emotions which are sent to test or transform us. When we use energy healing to clear these blocks, we are, as a result, able to live a more balanced, harmonious, and fulfilling life.

Even though I didn't really understand what it was all about, the whole idea of devoting some time to myself once a week for meditation and relaxation sounded just perfect! And so it began, a group guided meditation using the recording Cassandra had sent, during which she would send us all distance Reiki healing and afterwards we could share our experiences of what we felt, or experienced during that time. Mine was mostly a warm sensation of safety and security, with the odd vision in among the mix. Every single week was different though.

It really supported me through a time of very strange transition, I described it at the time as a feeling of being protected by a shield that allowed nothing to negatively affect me, or to penetrate my happy bubble. I bloody needed that, the few years running up to this time had been so tough, and undoubtedly taken their toll on my happy-go-lucky demeanour. I was tired, battling new situations in the attempt to co-parent with my ex every single day, and still recovering from a lot of emotional trauma. I loved the way it made me feel, I became untouchable.

During that year I also began another group coaching programme with Emily Hill, to help us manifest better business and lives of our own making, and a group healing session would follow our monthly calls too. It was a truly magical time when I really began to own my world, taking control AT LONG LAST and nothing could stop me. I remodelled my wedding stationery business during this time, bringing me more of the perfect kind of clients, life was getting easier again and I was really and truly happy in my newfound single mum life.

My journey began to inspire others as they could see the difference in me – I was lighter, less stressed, everything in my world just flowed and I knew I was deserving of it, having done this inner work.

As that year evolved I went from strength to strength, things just kept getting better and I felt empowered, magical even. So that when the time finally did come and I began considering dating again, I found my way simply and beautifully to the absolute love of my life, Bruce, to whom I am now engaged to be married. Okay, so it wasn't quite as straightforward as that but it really did happen at the absolute perfect time for me. He was everything I needed, and our worlds just blended seamlessly.

Towards the end of 2017 I had begun thinking about ways I wanted to start to do things differently, perhaps a course to get to understand it better – and in true Law of Attraction style, a lovely female Reiki Master nearby who I had met previously popped up in my Facebook feed offering a level 1 training session over 2 days. What? This truly felt like a sign, and as anyone in the know will tell you - when the student is ready, the teacher will come. I wanted to learn some new skills, and felt we could all benefit from me learning how to do it - who knew where it might lead? I had my 2 days of training with Esther, she explained the principles of it to me and we had the necessary healing sessions to accompany the Reiki attunement during which I saw my spirit animals, a unicorn, and a bear! It felt a bit unfamiliar to me, but during these sessions whatever you see is what you're supposed to see. Although I have not so far used my skills for more than helpful healing sessions at home, it helped my youngest no end with his anxiety and has helped both myself and Bruce no end during our rather complicated divorces!

The thing about energy work like Reiki healing is that it goes hand in hand with the universal laws because the more you believe in it helping you, the better you will feel. That is to say that the more positive energy you give an intention - the intention to heal in this case - the better benefit you will feel. I have written more about the Law of Attraction in another chapter so do feel free to check that out if you are curious. All of these things are there to help you in whatever way you feel you need, you can pick and choose whichever method feels right for you and just focus on that one.

What I have always loved about Reiki is that even if you don't believe you're going to benefit, you will still experience some kind of shift as a result of being receptive to it. You wouldn't ask someone to send you distance healing or to deliver hands-on Reiki to you if you didn't want or feel you needed it on some level, would you?

I would love to be able to continue on my journey and offer distance healing but I just haven't found the time and space to accommodate anything else just yet, life has been kind of busy, in the time since my Level 1 certification we have written 3 books, moved in together, both got divorced, got engaged, started new businesses, survived a global pandemic - and that's just a brief overview!

If I have piqued your interest in any way, perhaps it's something you could investigate for yourself and see. I wouldn't say it's a one cure fits all kind of approach. I am not saying Reiki will absolve you of all your ills overnight, but it is a powerful energy work that should at least be considered.

It's time you made more time for you!

PS: DON'T FORGET TO GRAB YOUR BONUS MATERIAL!

If you enjoyed the exercise at the end of the self-care section in chapter one, don't forget the bonus workbook I've created just for you!

Visit **bit.ly/YGTworkbook**

Where you can download your very own fully complimentary PDF workbook with simple exercises you can do to accompany each and every section of this book! They will help you get clear on what you *need* to do right now to better support yourself – and I'll be there cheering you on.

Reflections

It's time to take stock.

If you've read this whole book from cover to cover, (*wow, that's good going*) I wouldn't mind betting your head maybe feels a bit spinny. Where are you supposed to start? I've given you lots of suggestions but perhaps you're not sure what to do with any of them?

Hopefully, you have also that you feel inspired, motivated even, to start the process of putting yourself first, at last. Maybe you are already on that path but recognised yourself in the ideas found here, and now want to continue that momentum, to find yourself more fully.

Remember that journeys like this are not a 'linear' process, by which I mean there tends not to be a finishing line, but that any of the small steps lead to much bigger ones, those you once never dared to imagine.

Take a moment now.

Inside the workbook (link below, just in case) you will find a printable 'permission slip'. A promise to make to yourself, to take what you have learned, and make something beautiful happen from it. Permission to be more true to yourself. Permission to leave behind that uncertain person who has no faith in her own decisions. Permission to be *absolutely amazing*. Whatever you give yourself permission to be, do or have, do it with courage and confidence, and with my love - and remember my Heartfelt Approach always:

H is for Honour:

Give yourself credit for how far you've already come. Own the part you've had to play in your story and be proud of yourself. Honour where you're at now, ready to do the work.

E is for Embrace:

Encourage yourself in everything you already know is working, this belongs in your world. Know it is part of your future and begin to step fully in to everything else that feels more like you.

A is for Align:

Easily uncover wonderful opportunities which belong in your world, and watch those which are no longer relevant, fall away - feel your way into a more 'you' version of yourself.

R is for Realise:

Experience this plan taking beautiful shape, knowing it is all by design and not a happy accident. Pat yourself on the back for who you're becoming - and own it.

T is for Thrive:

You are now fully living your best life, with your best people, places and situations in tune with your beautiful being. Life is pretty bloody magnificent.

Feel more fully, **E**mbody you, **L**ove your life, **T**otal fulfilment.

You may recognise yourself somewhere in this - that's brilliant. If you are still thinking 'great, but what am I supposed to DO about it? I'm here to help. In fact I'd love nothing more. You can find my contact and social media details in my 'About the Author' section.

Remember, You've Got This!

With my Heartfelt Admiration,

Jacqueline x

Visit ***bit.ly/YGTworkbook***

To grab your very own fully complimentary PDF workbook with simple exercises to accompany each and every section of this book! They will help you get clear on what you need to do right now to better support yourself – and I'll be there cheering you on.

Useful Information

If any of the issues raised in this book affect you or someone in your life, remember help is always out there. Here is a handy list of some of the relevant organisations and help available.

www.thewellbeingthesis.org.uk
For plenty of info about the 7/11 breathing technique - they even have a free download available.

Here is a really useful website for a FREE health programme local to you:
www.efltrust.com/fitfans

Find out more from wikipedia about the various types of diets I have mentioned, as the science behind these is ever evolving:

Gluten and Casein free (GFCF diet):
wikipedia.org/wiki/Gluten-free,_casein-free_diet

Blood type diet:
wikipedia.org/wiki/Blood_type_diet

Food combining diet:
wikipedia.org/wiki/Food_combining

Self help group directory:
www.selfhelp.org.uk

Befriender Training:
www.befriending.co.uk

Counsellors:
www.counselling-directory.org.uk

Relate:
www.relate.org.uk

Bereaved Parents support:
The Compassionate Friends:
www.tcf.org.uk

SANDS: (Stillbirth and Neonatal Death Society):
www.sands.org.uk

Tuneless Choir:
www.tunelesschoir.com

Meditations:
Check out these apps:
Calm
Headspace

Disclaimer

This book is designed to provide helpful information on the subjects discussed. It is general reference information which should not be used to diagnose or treat any medical problem and is not intended as a substitute for consulting with a medical or professional practitioner.

For diagnosis of any medical problem, consult your own GP. The publisher and author are not responsible for any specific health or additional needs that may require medical supervision and are not liable for any damages or negative consequences from any treatment, action, application or preparation, to any person reading or following the information in this book.

References are provided for informational purposes only and do not consitute endorsement of any websites or other sources. Readers should be aware that the websites listed in this book may change.

About the Author

Jacqueline, who lives in Nottingham, England, has been described as a sparkling soul who lights up the room. She is often found looking thoughtful, pen in hand.

She is a Women's positivity and wellbeing author & coach. She helps women who have hit a mid-life stumbling block and find themselves searching for something more than 'just this'. Using her unique Heartfelt Approach, together they work to identify the cause of the unease, which is often linked to a lack of self-worth, and in a nurturing, supportive way helps them take steps to uncover the path to a more fulfilling life. She's really good at helping them learn to Flip the Script and understand that by focusing on more of the positives they can be set free from whatever isn't serving them and reap the rewards of living a life that they love.

Her mission is to help others see that there is always a light at the end of the tunnel, no matter what challenges they face.

When she isn't writing, coaching or sharing her journey, Jacqueline is always creative, spending time with her soulmate Bruce, maybe singing, dancing, or perhaps being a bit silly, and loves family time, too.

You can connect with me on:

- https://www.jacquelinekent.co.uk
- https://www.twitter.com/JKentCoaching
- https://www.facebook.com/groups/flipscript
- https://www.instagram.com/jacquelinekentcoaching

Subscribe to my newsletter:

- https://jacquelinekent.co.uk/subscribe

Also by Jacqueline Kent

My work is always written from the heart, to connect with women who need to know they always have a choice, no matter what trials they face.

Onward and Upward

Onward and Upward is a fascinating memoir of one woman's journey through motherhood, marriage and mayhem to her real-life happy ever after.

Follow Jacqueline on the ride of her life - she has been to hell and back many times over - as she makes a multitude of difficult decisions, triumphs through all kinds of adversity and strives for an 'ordinary' life. When she stumbles across her soulmate she finds her bliss, begins to understand her true purpose and takes a big, bold leap into her happy ending.

Her trials, torment and trauma are mingled with the happy and sad, the good and the bad (and the ugly), and this refreshing and powerful read will pull on your heartstrings, and make you laugh and cry. And when you learn about her happy ever after, you'll want to punch the air with delight!

The Girls Who Refused to Quit Volume 1

The Girls Who Refused to Quit shares the powerful, real-life journeys of 14 inspirational women. They have all overcome adversity and now want to make a difference with their stories.

Printed in Great Britain
by Amazon

43033551R00079